I0018985

Table of contents

Introduction

In this book we are going to introduce you to a remarkable electric pressure cooker – Instant Pot. We will tell you about its benefits and will list the recipes of appetizing and healthy dishes you can make with its help.

Instant Pot is truly a magical kitchen appliance, because it can do the work of seven other devices and can be programmed to complete the tasks. This appliance can substitute a slow cooker; a steamer; a pressure cooker; a porridge, rice or yoghurt maker; a pan for cooking sauté and the pot that will preserve the temperature of meals.

If you want to cook as a chef but do not wish to go through long-term studies, Instant Pot is the right choice for you! It will save you time and effort on education and will not take up much space in the kitchen. All you have to do is just study its functions, learn how to use it and follow the recipes provided. You will also get much room for creativity and are welcome to come up with your own recipes after you are comfortable with the basic ones. Free your imagination and dive into the exciting world of cooking with this amazing appliance!

Taking Care of Instant Pot

Let us give you a few hints as to how to care for this handy device to keep it going for even longer time. First of all, it is best to clean it every time after food preparation. You can do this either manually, using a piece of fabric, or implementing a dishwasher. Wash the detachable parts of the appliance in the dishwasher to eliminate any grease left. Remember to disconnect the cooker from electricity prior to taking out its units. Put only dry details back into the cooker, never use them wet.

If you would like to make sure that the cooker does not contain any foreign smell, you can clean it with vinegar. Use the following recommendations: put a little lemon juice, vinegar and water into the Instant Pot and heat the mixture up in "Steam" mode. This way you will get rid of any smell or bacteria that might have stayed in the cooker. You do not need to wash the appliance after this procedure.

Instant Pot and Slow Cooker Comparison

Now we would like to focus on the advantages this device possesses and tell you why it is beneficial for you to use it.

Let us see why you might want to prefer this appliance to the slow cooker. These devices are alike in many ways, but they also have some fundamental differences.

If you have ever cooked in a slow cooker, you know that it uses a low temperature range, which is not higher than 200°F. It takes the slow cooker approximately four hours to prepare the meal, while an electric pressure appliance cooks the dish in less than one hour. Electric pressure cooker runs at higher temperatures, ranging from 239°F to 244°F. Thus, Instant Pot as an electric pressure device is much quicker than a slow cooker and spends much less electric energy on preparing the same meal. It is important that Instant Pot is firmly closed under pressure, and it does not let any air streams or smells out, like a slow cooker does. There are no smells in the house when you are cooking with Instant Pot, which is also its benefit. Instant Pot also removes the toxins from the products due to its operating temperature, which is higher than boiling point.

The Meals That Can Be Prepared With the Instant Pot

The operation buttons on the cooker's panel indicate the types of meals that can be cooked in the pot. If you press these buttons, you will set your dishes to cook for a programmed amount of time.

Multigrain option allows you to cook solid grains, for example, brown rice. If you would like to make porridge out of the grain or cereal, you can use **Congee/Porridge** mode. **Sauté/ Browning** function permits you to make sauté with the Instant Pot lid open. Cooking different kinds of beans is convenient at **Beans/ Chili** regime. **Soup** option is a great one to prepare delicious soups and broths. Instant Pot can also perform the functions of the **slow cooker**, and in such cases it does not apply pressure. The button for this regime is named accordingly. Meat and stews can be made with the help of **Meat/Stew** function. There is also a special button for cooking **rice**. Vegetables can be steamed at **Steam** mode. All poultry dishes will turn out perfectly if you use a **Poultry** regime. **Yogurt** button speaks for itself and is also very helpful. Each function automatically switches to **Keep warm** option after the dish is prepared.

You can see that your cooking opportunities are endless with this device: you can cook all kinds of fruits and vegetables, meat, seafood, grains, etc. The choice of dishes you can make with it is much wider than your options without it. The oven or even other pressure cookers will not substitute this smart appliance.

If you use Instant Pot, you do not need to keep track of time and implement a timer, like you had to do while using a regular pressure cooker. It is certainly possible for you to set the time of supporting pressure manually, if you want to differ it. There is also a nice delayed cooking option in this appliance, which allows you to plan the meal you are going to make beforehand.

The Advantages of Instant Pot

Let us sum up the most significant benefits of this irreplaceable appliance.

First of all, the pot is very user-friendly because of the pre-programmed function buttons for all types of meals. It allows postponing meal preparation for up to 24 hours.

Cooking with Instant Pot you save your time significantly, because food is prepared quickly due to high temperature. Therefore, you also save energy, since the appliance does not work for hours. You do not consume as much electricity as you had to when you used an oven, steamer, stove and boiling pot. Statistics show that using Instant Pot permits a consumer to lower electricity spending by more than two times.

Another feature that makes Instant Pot nature-friendly is that it does not allow air flow, since it is isolated very well. The internal cooking pot is surrounded by a double layer of air pockets, which separate it from the environment. This means that the pot does not spend unnecessary energy and does not heat up the exterior instead of the meal. All of the heat is focused on the food being prepared and none of it goes outside. It is another advantage of Instant Pot over regular pressure cookers. Besides, due to this feature all the fragrance stays with the food being cooked, instead of attracting the attention of your family members and neighbors. The work of the device is quiet and it does not make noise.

It is also worth mentioning that Instant Pot heating system is designed to support the needed level of pressure. The cooker is not constantly heated up, it only warms up to keep up the mandatory pressure mark.

Since the appliance is well isolated, its level of steaming is about 70 percent lower than the one of other devices. This ensures that you spend much less water on cooking and you do not have to stay in a misty and hot kitchen.

It is certainly pleasant that this cooker does not make your kitchen dirty, because you do not spill anything and the food does not boil excessively. Having this device, you can reduce the number of kitchen tools since you do not need them, and this way you will avoid mess and excessive money spending.

Speaking of health and the influence of Instant Pot on food products, the meals turn out soft and full of all the crucial vitamins and elements. The dishes cooked in the pot remain fragrant and they are well cooked on all layers. Because of the fact that you do not use much water, all the useful elements stay within food and they are not washed away by water. The absence of steam leakage helps vegetables save their colors and chemicals.

Not only vegetables, but also firm products, such as meat and ribs become tender in Instant Pot. According to customer experiences, the meat prepared in this cooker is easy to chew on, and legumes and grains turn out to be delicate and fully cooked.

The undeniable advantage of Instant Pot is that the heat generated by the cooker is spread evenly and profoundly inside the products, and it does not matter if there is much food in the device or not. The cooking process is steady and does not depend on the amount of water or products in the pot because of smart programming. Due to this fact Instant Pot produces high-quality and pleasant tasting dishes.

We hope that you will enjoy using your cooker and will give a try to the recipes we have provided for you! These nourishing and yummy dishes will be the adornment of your table.

Hard Boiled Eggs

These eggs are a great choice for a breakfast! Not only are they nourishing, but also quick and easy to make.

Prep time: 1 minute
Cooking time: 15 minutes
Servings: 6-8 eggs

Ingredients:
- 6-8 big eggs just taken out of the fridge
- 1 cup of cool water

Directions:
1. Put the eggs into the Instant Pot.
2. Pour 1 cup of cool water into the pressure cooker and put a rack inside it. Locate 6 to 8 big eggs on the rack and close the lid securely.
3. You can choose to cook the eggs under either high or low pressure. For high pressure select the time "8 minutes" and fast release. For low pressure set the time "12 minutes" and fast release.
4. When the cooking time is up, open the lid with care.
5. If you need to serve the eggs all at once, it is best to peel them under cold water stream from the tap. They are ready to be served when they are peeled.
6. If you do not want to serve the eggs as soon as they are ready, fill the bowl with cold water and let them cool down for approximately 5 minutes.

Nutrition:
- Calories: 72
- Fat: 5g
- Cholesterol: 186mg
- Carbohydrates: 0.4g
- Protein: 6.3g

Oatmeal with Vanilla and Cinnamon

This appetizing dish will leave nobody impartial. It is a wonderful mix of taste and value!

Prep time: 2 minutes
Cooking time: 3 minutes
Servings: 4

Ingredients:
- 2 cups of water
- 1 dash of sea salt
- 1 cup of cashew milk with no sugar
- 1 cup of porridge oats
- 1 teaspoon of vanilla extract
- 1 teaspoon of cinnamon
- 0.3 cup of cut dried cranberries
- 0.25 cup of cut dried walnuts
- 1 or 2 tablespoons of agave nectar (can be substituted with honey)

Directions:
1. Put oats, water, milk and salt into the Instant Pot.
2. Close the lid carefully.
3. Choose the "Manual" mode and set the time for 3 minutes.
4. Upon hearing the sound signal, let the oatmeal stay in the Instant Pot until the pressure reduces and you will not have to force the lid open. You may have to wait for 10 to 15 minutes.
5. Add other ingredients to the oatmeal: cinnamon, vanilla, agave nectar (or honey), cranberries and walnuts. Make the dish as sweet as you want it to be.
6. You may add supplementary walnuts or cranberries according to your taste.
7. Oatmeal can be stored in the fridge during 4 days and heated up in the microwave.

Nutrition:
- Calories: 161
- Fat: 6.5g
- Cholesterol: 0mg
- Carbohydrates: 22g
- Protein: 4.6g

Oatmeal from the Mix of Berries

The unforgettable flavor of berries will make your breakfast a very pleasant one! Both grown-ups and children will love this dish.

Prep time: 7 minutes
Cooking time: 7 minutes
Servings: 6

Ingredients:
- 1 cup of blackberries
- 0.25 cup of strawberries
- 4 cups of water
- 2 cups of porridge oats
- 2 tablespoons of honey
- 1 teaspoon of brown sugar
- 2 tablespoons of white sugar

Directions:
1. Put the oats in the Instant Pot and cover them with water.
2. Add some white sugar and honey to the dish.
3. Mix it up slightly and close the lid.
4. Use the "Porridge" mode and let the dish prepare for 7 minutes, or for as long as the oats producer suggests.
5. While the oatmeal is being cooked, cut the strawberries and blackberries and collect them in one bowl.
6. Supplement them with brown sugar and honey according to your taste.
7. Blend the ingredients thoroughly.
8. When the dish is prepared, you may put it into the serving plates.
9. Place the mix of berries on top of the oatmeal.
10. The porridge is ready for serving.

Nutrition:
- Calories: 141
- Fat: 1.1g
- Carbohydrates: 32.53g
- Protein: 2g

Light Oatmeal with Turmeric and Pistachios

You will definitely enjoy this soft and fragrant porridge. This exotic meal is a great source of vitamins!

Prep time: 5 minutes
Cooking time: 7 minutes
Servings: 4

Ingredients:
- 1 cup of coconut milk
- 2 cups of almond milk
- 1 cup of porridge oats
- 1 teaspoon of turmeric
- 3 tablespoons of pistachio nuts
- 1 teaspoon of salt
- 0.3 cup of brown sugar
- 0.25 teaspoon of cardamom
- 1 teaspoon of raisins
- 0.5 teaspoon of lemon zest
- 2 tablespoons of lemon juice

Directions:
1. Put the following ingredients into the Instant Pot and mix them: coconut milk, almond milk, oats, turmeric and pistachios.
2. Complete this combination with cardamom, lemon juice, lemon zest, sugar and salt.
3. Top the meal with raisins and mix it thoroughly.
4. Close the lid and turn on the "Porridge" regime.
5. Let the dish prepare for 7 minutes.
6. When it is ready, stir the meal with care.
7. Now the dish is ready to be served. Fill the serving dishes with this delicious and healthy oatmeal!

Nutrition:
- Calories: 351
- Fat: 19.1g
- Carbohydrates: 44.75g
- Protein: 5g

Scrambled Eggs with Bacon and Greenery

This traditional dish is easy to make and it will be an energetic start of your morning! It will keep you full for a long time, and takes no more than 15 minutes to cook.

Prep time: 5 minutes
Cooking time: 12 minutes
Servings: 5

Ingredients:
- 7 eggs
- 0.5 cup of milk
- 1 tablespoon of basil
- 1 tablespoon of butter
- 1 teaspoon of salt
- 1 teaspoon of paprika
- 0.25 cup of fresh cut parsley
- 4 oz. of bacon
- 1 tablespoon of cilantro

Directions:
1. Beat the eggs in the bowl and whip them carefully.
2. Add 0.5 cup of milk, a pinch of salt, paprika, basil and cilantro to the eggs.
3. Mix the eggs and the ingredients added.
4. Cut parsley and bacon finely.
5. Turn on the Instant Pot and use "Sauté" mode.
6. Cut the bacon and put it into the Instant Pot.
7. Let it cook for 3 minutes.
8. Add whipped eggs to the bacon and let the dish cook for 5 more minutes.
9. Stir the mixture (it is best to use a wooden spoon).
10. Spread cut parsley over the dish and let it cook for 4 more minutes.
11. Upon readiness take the eggs out of the pressure cooker.
12. The meal is ready to be served!

Nutrition:
- Calories: 290
- Fat: 23.4g
- Carbohydrates: 4.53g
- Protein: 16g

Soft Boiled Eggs with Paprika and Lettuce

Those of you who love simplicity and good taste will enjoy this dish. Lettuce will make it succulent and will add flavor to it.

Prep time: 15 minutes
Cooking time: 15 minutes
Servings: 6

Ingredients:
- 2 cups of water
- 4 eggs
- 1 avocado
- 1 sweet pepper
- 1 teaspoon of paprika
- 1 teaspoon of salt
- 1 teaspoon of ground black pepper
- 3 tablespoons of cream
- 3 oz. of the leaves of lettuce

Directions:
1. Pour the water into the Instant Pot and put the eggs inside it. Close the lid.
2. Turn on the "Pressure" mode and let the eggs cook for 15 minutes.
3. Prepare the ice bath.
4. Take the eggs out of the pressure cooker and put them into the ice bath.
5. Cut the avocado and clear the sweet pepper from the seeds.
6. Cut the sweet pepper into slices.
7. Take the eggs from the bath, peel and cut them.
8. Place all the cut components into the bowl and mix them.
9. Spread ground black pepper, salt and paprika over the dish, and stir it once again.
10. Wash the leaves of the lettuce and put them on the plate.
11. Put the mixture on lettuce and cover the dish with a cream.
12. Now the beautiful dish is ready to be served!

Nutrition:
- Calories: 168
- Fat: 12.9g
- Carbohydrates: 6.75g
- Protein: 7g

Apricot Soufflé with Cream

This enticing meal can be served both cooled and hot. You will get a wonderful dessert with cottage cheese in just 20 minutes!

Prep time: 10 minutes
Cooking time: 20 minutes
Servings: 6

Ingredients:
- 1 cup of cream
- 3 eggs
- 6 oz. of cottage cheese
- 1 tablespoon of sour cream
- 2 tablespoons of sugar
- 4 tablespoons of butter
- 1 teaspoon of vanilla extract
- 0.3 cup of dried apricots

Directions:
1. Whip the 3 eggs and add a sour cream.
2. Put cottage cheese into the bowl and use a manual mixer to mix it.
3. Complement cottage cheese with the whipped eggs, sour cream, butter, vanilla and sugar.
4. Stir the mixture until it is smooth and does not contain firm pieces.
5. Add dried apricots to the mass and mix it carefully.
6. Place the mass into the Instant Pot and shut the lid.
7. Turn on the "Stew" regime and prepare the meal for 20 minutes.
8. Upon readiness, give the dish some time to cool down.
9. Now it is ready to be served!

Nutrition:
- Calories: 266
- Fat: 21.1g
- Carbohydrates: 11.72g
- Protein: 8g

Omelet with Parmesan Cheese and Spinach

This tender dish will suit those of you who like omelets. The greenery and cheese will add exotic flavor to it.

Prep time: 6 minutes
Cooking time: 6 minutes
Servings: 5

Ingredients:
- 8 eggs
- 2 cups of spinach
- 0.5 cup of milk
- 1 tablespoon of olive oil
- 1 teaspoon of salt
- 1 teaspoon of ground black pepper
- 4 oz. of parmesan cheese

Directions:
1. Beat all the eggs into the bowl and whip them.
2. Cut some spinach and add it to the eggs.
3. Complete the mixture with olive oil, salt, ground black pepper and milk, and stir it.
4. Grate the 4 oz. of parmesan cheese and set it aside for a while.
5. Put the mix of eggs and other ingredients into the Instant Pot.
6. Choose the "Steam" regime and let the meal cook for 6 minutes.
7. When ready, take it out of the pressure cooker and place on the serving dish.
8. Spread the Parmesan you have grated over the omelet.
9. Enjoy your meal!

Nutrition:
- Calories: 336
- Fat: 21g
- Carbohydrates: 13g
- Protein: 25g

Pieces of Pastry with Cheese and Bacon

This tempting dish can be served hot and warm. Let yourself enjoy its aroma and exquisite taste!

Prep time: 6 minutes
Cooking time: 20 minutes
Servings: 8

Ingredients:
- 6 oz. of bacon
- 10 oz. of hard cheese
- 1 teaspoon of oregano
- 1 teaspoon of butter
- 2 egg yolks
- 5 oz. of puff pastry
- 1 teaspoon of sesame seeds

Directions:
1. Cut the bacon and hard cheese (it is best to slice cheese into cubes).
2. Roll the puff pastry using the rolling pin.
3. Whip two egg yolks.
4. Spread sesame seeds and oregano on top of them.
5. Cut the rolled puff pastry into squares and fill each square with butter.
6. Wrap the cubes of cheese into the pieces of bacon.
7. Put cheese and bacon into pastry squares.
8. Shape the pieces of dough with cheese and bacon inside them.
9. Put the egg yolk on top of those pieces.
10. Place the dough bites into the Instant Pot.
11. Shut the lid securely and use the "Steam" regime.
12. Let the meal cook for 20 minutes.
13. When the time is up, the dish is ready to be served all at once.

Nutrition:
- Calories: 321
- Fat: 24g
- Carbohydrates: 11g
- Protein: 16g

Millet and Pumpkin Porridge

The delectable porridge of soft and juicy pumpkin is useful for your body. We suggest using a sweet sort of pumpkin if you want your porridge to be sweet.

Prep time: 10 minutes
Cooking time: 15 minutes
Servings: 5

Ingredients:
- 1 cup of water
- 1 cup of milk
- 1 pound of sweet pumpkin
- 0.3 cup of millet
- 2 teaspoons of brown sugar
- 1 teaspoon of cinnamon
- 0.5 teaspoon of cardamom
- 0.5 teaspoon of turmeric

Directions:
1. Clean the pumpkin, peel it and cut it into pieces.
2. Place it into the Instant Pot, covering it with water and milk.
3. Add brown sugar, turmeric, cardamom and cinnamon to the pumpkin.
4. Complete the mixture with millet and stir it carefully.
5. Shut the lid and set the regime "Rice" for cooking.
6. Let the meal cook for 15 minutes.
7. Once the dish is ready, use a manual blender to mix up the porridge until it reaches a smooth condition.
8. Fill the serving dishes with the luscious porridge!

Nutrition:
- Calories: 610
- Fat: 47g
- Carbohydrates: 28g
- Protein: 30g

Delicious Eggs in Tomato Sauce

This nourishing dish is great for breakfast! Make it for the whole family and start your day with the mix of vegetables and eggs.

Prep time: 5 minutes
Cooking time: 5 minutes
Servings: 4

Ingredients:
- 3 fresh tomatoes of average size
- 4 eggs
- 1 red onion
- 1 tablespoon of olive oil
- 1 tablespoon of dill (it is better to use fresh one)
- 1 teaspoon of salt
- 0.5 teaspoon of white pepper
- 0.5 teaspoon of paprika

Directions:
1. Cover the inside of the cooking bowl with olive oil evenly.
2. Beat the eggs into the cooking bowl.
3. Mix white pepper, paprika, dill and salt in another bowl.
4. Cut the red onion.
5. Slice the tomatoes into small pieces and mix them with onion.
6. Cover the eggs with tomato and onion mixture.
7. Add the condiments to the eggs and place the mix into the Instant Pot.
8. Shut the lid and turn on the "Steam" regime.
9. Prepare the dish for 5 minutes.
10. Take it out of the pressure cooker and let it cool down for a short while.
11. The dish is ready to be served!

Nutrition:
- Calories: 194
- Fat: 14g
- Carbohydrates: 8.5g
- Protein: 10g

Spicy Instant Bread with Eggs

These buns with eggs and spices are outstanding! They will be an original breakfast for the whole family.

Prep time: 8 minutes
Cooking time: 10 minutes
Servings: 6

Ingredients:
- 4 eggs
- 9 oz. of white bread
- 7 oz. of hard cheese
- 1 tablespoon of butter
- 0.5 teaspoon of sour cream
- 0.5 teaspoon of hot chili pepper
- 1 teaspoon of salt

Directions:
1. Slice the bread into large cubes and make cuts in the bread pieces.
2. Mix the sour cream, salt and hot chili pepper in a separate bowl.
3. Place a piece of butter into the Instant Pot.
4. Beat the eggs into the cubes of bread and place them into the Instant Pot.
5. Cover the meal with the mix of condiments.
6. Grate the cheese and cover the bread with it.
7. Close the lid and turn on the "Steam" mode.
8. Let the dish cook for 10 minutes.
9. Let it cool down a little bit and then serve it!

Nutrition:
- Calories: 265
- Fat: 12g
- Carbohydrates: 23g
- Protein: 15g

Tender Whipped Eggs with Vegetables

This delightful dish will suit the vegetarians. It is a healthy way to start your day!

Prep time: 10 minutes
Cooking time: 15 minutes
Servings: 6

Ingredients:
- 10 eggs
- 1 cup of milk (either soy or cow milk)
- 1 sweet pepper
- 3 fresh tomatoes
- 1 zucchini
- 5 oz. of asparagus
- 0.5 cup of cilantro
- 0.5 of jalapeno pepper
- 1 teaspoon of ground black pepper
- 1 teaspoon of salt
- 1 tablespoon of butter

Directions:
1. Beat all the eggs in the bowl and whip them well.
2. Add milk, salt, black pepper and butter to the mixture and stir it.
3. Cut the tomatoes, zucchini, asparagus and cilantro.
4. Free the sweet pepper from the seeds and slice it as well.
5. Cut the jalapeno pepper.
6. Put the egg and condiment mixture into the Instant Pot.
7. Cover the eggs with sliced vegetables.
8. Set the pressure cooker to "Steam" regime and let the dish prepare for 15 minutes.
9. When the time has passed, the vegetable dish is ready. You are welcome to taste it right away!

Nutrition:
- Calories: 284
- Fat: 20g
- Carbohydrates: 10g
- Protein: 18g

Piquant Eggs in Rice Wine

This recipe originated in Asia and lets us enjoy the exotic rice wine sauce. If you want to start your morning with something unusual, this dish is the right choice!

Prep time: 10 minutes
Cooking time: 5 minutes
Servings: 5

Ingredients:
- 5 boiled eggs
- 0.5 cup of water
- 1 teaspoon of chili flakes
- 1 teaspoon of salt
- 0.3 cup of soy sauce
- 1 teaspoon of cilantro
- 1 tablespoon of lemon juice
- 1 tablespoon of sugar
- 2 tablespoons of sweet rice wine (mirin)
- 0.5 teaspoon of ground black pepper

Directions:
1. Peel the boiled eggs and put them into the Instant Pot.
2. Use the mixing bowl to mix the following ingredients: cilantro, soy sauce, ground black pepper, lemon juice, rice wine, water, chili flakes and salt. Mix the solution until it is smooth.
3. Pour the solution into the pressure cooker and stir it slightly.
4. Shut the Instant Pot and set the "Meat/Stew" regime.
5. Let the dish prepare for 5 minutes.
6. Take the meal out into a glass bowl and let it linger there until it has cooled won.
7. Once the eggs are cool, you can serve them or put them into the fridge.

Nutrition:
- Calories: 189
- Fat: 13g
- Carbohydrates: 8g
- Protein: 10g

Rice Stewed in Rich Cream

This dish is very appetizing! You will be satisfied, especially if you serve it straight from the Instant Pot.

Prep time: 10 minutes
Cooking time: 15 minutes
Servings: 3

Ingredients:
- 1 cup of long-grain rice
- 1 cup of thick cream
- 1 cup of milk
- 0.25 cup of water
- 1 teaspoon of salt
- 4 tablespoons of brown sugar
- 1 teaspoon of cinnamon

Directions:
1. Place the rice into the Instant Pot.
2. Cover it with thick cream of your choice, your favorite milk, and water.
3. Whip all these ingredients carefully and complement them with cinnamon, brown sugar and salt.
4. Make sure you have an indistinguishable mixture.
5. Switch on the Instant Pot "Rice" regime and let the dish prepare for 15 minutes.
6. Open the lid and mix the meal thoroughly.
7. Now the dish is ready to be served.
8. You might want to serve it hot for better taste.

Nutrition:
- Calories: 420
- Fat: 19g
- Carbohydrates: 53g
- Protein: 8g

Heavenly Yoghurt with the Seeds of Chia

This meal is tasty and useful at the same time. The seeds of chia are rich in super-useful microelements, which will bring health to your organism.

Prep time: 5 minutes
Cooking time: 7 minutes
Servings: 3

Ingredients:
- 1 cup of water
- 1 cup of chia seeds
- 1 cup of Greek yoghurt
- 2 apples
- 1 tablespoon of honey
- 1 teaspoon of lemon zest
- 1 teaspoon of cloves
- 0.5 teaspoon of cinnamon
- 0.25 teaspoon of salt

Directions:
1. Mix the Greek yoghurt with water in a bowl.
2. Place an obtained mixture into the Instant Pot and spray it with chia seeds.
3. Stir it thoroughly and complement with cinnamon, honey, lemon zest, salt and cloves.
4. Wash the apples, peel them and cut them into fine pieces.
5. Put the sliced apples into the pressure cooker.
6. Mix up the solution to make it smooth.
7. Close the lid and set it to "Steam" regime.
8. Let the dish cook for 7 minutes.
9. When ready, stir the dish tenderly and take it out of the pressure cooker.
10. This meal is great when served hot!

Nutrition:
- Calories: 417
- Fat: 19g
- Carbohydrates: 50g
- Protein: 17g

Stewed Chicken with Cheese

This dish is enjoyable when it is both hot and cooled. Use your favorite sort of hard cheese and the cream of your choice to meet your dietary needs.

Prep time: 15 minutes
Cooking time: 30 minutes
Servings: 6

Ingredients:
- The yolks of 4 eggs
- 1 pound of chicken fillet
- 1 onion
- 1 cup of cream
- 10 oz. of hard cheese
- 1 tablespoon of butter
- 1 tablespoon of lemon juice
- 1 teaspoon of salt
- 0.5 teaspoon of ground black pepper

Directions:
1. Slice the chicken fillet into pieces and coat them with lemon juice, salt and ground black pepper.
2. Stir the chicken pieces and make sure they have soaked in the condiments well.
3. Grate some hard cheese.
4. Peel the onion and cut it into small pieces.
5. Add butter to onion and mix it up.
6. Put an obtained mixture into the Instant Pot.
7. Add some cream and the cheese you have grated to it.
8. Set the Instant Pot to the "Poultry" mode.
9. The dish should cook for a half an hour.
10. When it is ready, let it cool down for a short time.
11. The meal is now ready to be served!

Nutrition:
- Calories: 424
- Fat: 28g
- Carbohydrates: 27g
- Protein: 18g

Crispy Vanilla Toasts

These crisp vanilla toasts will win your heart! The dish is sweet and very pleasant to taste.

Prep time: 10 minutes
Cooking time: 8 minutes
Servings: 7

Ingredients:
- 1 cup of milk
- 4 raw eggs
- 1 pound of white bread of your choice
- 3 tablespoons of brown sugar
- 1 teaspoon of vanilla sugar
- 1 tablespoon of butter

Directions:
1. Cut the white bread.
2. Beat the raw eggs into the bowl and supplement them with milk.
3. Whip the solution and sweeten it with brown sugar.
4. Add some vanilla sugar to the egg solution and blend it thoroughly. Make sure that all the sugar has integrated into the mixture.
5. Dip the pieces of white bread into this mixture.
6. Put some butter into the pressure cooker and let its sides be covered in butter.
7. Put the bread covered in mixture into the Instant Pot.
8. Choose the "Sauté" option and cook the dish for 4 minutes on every side.
9. Once the toasts are ready on both sides, take them out of the pressure cooker and let them cool down somewhat.
10. Now the warm toasts are ready to be served.

Nutrition:
- Calories: 274
- Fat: 10g
- Carbohydrates: 33g
- Protein: 13g

Savory Banana Sandwiches

Your family will adore these sandwiches with marshmallows and banana. They are good both for regular breakfast and for special occasions.

Prep time: 5 minutes
Cooking time: 6 minutes
Servings: 4

Ingredients:
- 1 banana
- 5 oz. of white bread of your choice
- 6 oz. of marshmallow
- 2 tablespoons of butter
- 1 teaspoon of vanilla sugar
- 1 teaspoon of cinnamon

Directions:
1. Take off the banana peel and cut the fruit into pieces.
2. Slice the marshmallows.
3. Cut the white bread and cover it with butter on both sides.
4. Spread some brown and vanilla sugar on the bread.
5. Put sliced marshmallows and the pieces of banana on top of the bread slices.
6. Put the bread into the Instant Pot and shut the lid.
7. Turn on the "Meat/Stew" mode and let the meal cook for 3 minutes on every side.
8. Take the sandwiches out and let them cool down for some time.
9. The sweet dish is ready to be tasted now!

Nutrition:
- Calories: 360
- Fat: 10g
- Carbohydrates: 66g
- Protein: 6g

Cocoa Porridge with Almonds

This exquisite dish can be cooked from any type of flour. Chocolate and cocoa will make the meal your child's favorite!

Prep time: 10 minutes
Cooking time: 13 minutes
Servings: 3

Ingredients:
- 1 cup of water
- 1 cup of corn flour
- 0.3 cup of milk
- 3 tablespoons of cocoa powder
- 3 tablespoons of almonds
- 1 tablespoon of brown sugar
- 1 teaspoon of vanilla sugar
- 1 tablespoon of butter
- 1 tablespoon of dark chocolate
- 1 teaspoon of sesame seeds
- 1 teaspoon of raisins
- 1 teaspoon of olive oil

Directions:
1. Crack the almonds.
2. Mix up brown and vanilla sugar, dark chocolate and cocoa powder in a bowl. Blend the mixture well.
3. Spread the olive oil inside the Instant Pot to make sure the sides are covered.
4. Place corn flour into the Instant Pot and add the mixture of cocoa powder, vanilla sugar and chocolate.
5. Top that with cracked almonds, milk, water and raisins.
6. Use a wooden spoon to mix up the mixture.
7. Close the lid and turn on the "High pressure" regime.
8. It takes 13 minutes to cook the dish.
9. After that time blend the porridge thoroughly with the spoon to make sure there are no clumps inside.
10. Put the chocolate mix into serving plates and enjoy it!

Nutrition:
- Calories: 280
- Fat: 10g
- Carbohydrates: 47g
- Protein: 6g

Sweetened Semolina with Turmeric and Clove

The splendid fast-cooked porridge will remind you of your childhood and will be ready in just 12 minutes.

Prep time: 5 minutes
Cooking time: 12 minutes
Servings: 6

Ingredients:
- 2 cups of milk (or cream of your choice, if you wish to make the dish more nourishing)
- 2 cups of semolina
- 3 tablespoons of sugar
- 1 teaspoon of salt
- 3 tablespoons of butter
- 1 teaspoon of clove
- 0.5 teaspoon of vanilla extract
- 0.5 teaspoon of turmeric

Directions:
1. Put the milk, salt, sugar, clove, turmeric and vanilla extract into the Instant Pot.
2. Blend the mixture.
3. Turn on the "Pressure" regime of the Instant Pot.
4. Prepare the mixture for 10 minutes.
5. After that time add semolina to the mixture. Stir it well and close the lid again.
6. Let the meal cook for 2 more minutes.
7. Take the porridge out of the Instant Pot and let it cool down slightly.
8. The dish is now ready to be served, so eat it while it is warm!

Nutrition:
- Calories: 320
- Fat: 9g
- Carbohydrates: 48g
- Protein: 10g

Amazing Pudding with Rice and Cinnamon

This meal is a true masterpiece and is very tasty while it is still hot! You will enjoy its soft texture and pleasant flavor.

Prep time: 10 minutes
Cooking time: 15 minutes
Servings: 4

Ingredients:
- 1 cup of long grain rice
- 4 tablespoons of sugar
- 2 cups of milk
- 2 tablespoons of cream
- 1 teaspoon of salt
- 1 teaspoon of butter
- 1 teaspoon of cinnamon
- 1 teaspoon of ground cardamom

Directions:
1. Put the rice, sugar, salt and milk into the Instant Pot and blend them thoroughly.
2. Cloe the lid and turn on the "Porridge" mode.
3. Let the dish cook for 15 minutes.
4. After the time has passed, let the rice sit in the Pot for a little while.
5. Afterwards open the cooker and complete the rice with cardamom, butter, cinnamon and cream.
6. Use a wooden spoon (it is the healthiest material) to stir the dish.
7. Put the cooked rice pudding on serving plates.
8. You may add the jam of your taste if you desire the pudding to be extra sweet.
9. The dish is ready to be served!

Nutrition:
- Calories: 300
- Fat: 8g
- Carbohydrates: 51g
- Protein: 8g

Delicate Buckwheat Porridge with Dried Fruits

This food item is rich in useful microelements and can be cooked every morning. It is one of the ways to alter the good old buckwheat porridge you are used to.

Prep time: 10 minutes
Cooking time: 20 minutes
Servings: 3

Ingredients:
- 1 cup of buckwheat
- 1 cup of milk
- 1 cup of almond milk
- 2 tablespoons of honey
- 2 tablespoons of butter
- 1 teaspoon of vanilla extract
- 0.5 teaspoon of ground ginger
- 0.3 cup of raisins
- 0.25 cup of dried apricots

Directions:
1. Pour regular milk and almond milk into one bowl.
2. Add some ginger, honey and vanilla extract to the milk. Use the honey of your choice.
3. Blend the milk and the additives with care.
4. Supplement the mixture with some butter and stir it once again.
5. Grind dried apricots and raisins.
6. Place the milk mixture into the Instant Pot.
7. Complete it with a cup of buckwheat and the dried ground fruits you have prepared.
8. Turn on the "Porridge" mode of the pressure cooker.
9. Let the dish cook for 20 minutes.
10. Upon readiness open up the lid and stir the meal slightly.
11. Now the porridge is ready to be served and tasted.

Nutrition:
- Calories: 283
- Fat: 12g
- Carbohydrates: 41g
- Protein: 5g

Nutrient Grain Mixture

The complex of various grain types enriched with chicken broth makes this dish very healthful. You can have it for breakfast or brunch.

Prep time: 10 minutes
Cooking time: 30 minutes
Servings: 5

Ingredients:
- 3 cups of chicken broth
- 0.5 cup of brown rice
- 0.5 cup of white rice
- 0.5 cup of millet
- 3 tablespoons of butter
- 1 sliced onion
- 1 teaspoon of salt
- 3 oz. of dates

Directions:
1. Prepare a mixing dish and put all the three kinds of grain there: brown rice, white rice and millet.
2. Put some sliced onion and salt into the bowl.
3. Cut the dates and spread them in the bowl as well.
4. Place the grain with the additives into the pressure cooker and pour chicken broth into it.
5. Blend the mixture accurately and cover it with the lid.
6. Switch on the "Multigrain" regime of the Instant Pot.
7. Let the meal be prepared for 30 minutes.
8. After that period of time take the mixture out of the Instant Pot and relocate it into the mixing dish.
9. Complete it with some butter and stir it thoroughly.
10. Now you are welcome to serve the dish and enjoy it!

Nutrition:
- Calories: 382
- Fat: 10g
- Carbohydrates: 64g
- Protein: 9g

Honeyed Pumpkin Mush

Small children will enjoy this soft dish, especially if they like pumpkin. It is wholesome and has a pleasant taste.

Prep time: 10 minutes
Cooking time: 20 minutes
Servings: 4

Ingredients:
- 1 pound of pumpkin
- 0.5 cup of water
- 0.25 cup of raisins
- 2 tablespoons of cream of your choice
- 1 tablespoon of honey
- 1 teaspoon of butter
- 1 teaspoon of cinnamon
- 0.5 teaspoon of vanilla extract

Directions:
1. Clean the pumpkin, peel it and cut it into pieces.
2. Put the sliced vegetable into the Instant Pot.
3. Complement it with butter, cinnamon, vanilla extract and water.
4. Close the lid firmly and set the "Pressure" mode.
5. Let the meal cook for 20 minutes.
6. Afterwards take the food out of the pressure cooker and put it into the blender.
7. Make sure to blend it well until the mixture reminds of puree.
8. Mix the raisins and the cream of your choice into the blend.
9. Add some honey and stir the dish once again.
10. Let the meal cool down a little bit and serve it while it is warm.

Nutrition:
- Calories: 690
- Fat: 58g
- Carbohydrates: 22g
- Protein: 34g

Cauliflower Pieces in Tomato Juice

This syrupy and health-giving dish is wonderful for breakfast. It will give you the necessary vitamins and the energy resource.

Prep time: 10 minutes
Cooking time: 30 minutes
Servings: 4

Ingredients:
- 1 pound of cauliflower
- 2 eggs
- 1 white onion
- 0.25 cup of tomato juice
- 3 tablespoons of flour
- 2 tablespoons of semolina
- 1 teaspoon of olive oil
- 1 teaspoon of salt
- 1 teaspoon of chicken broth

Directions:
1. Cut the cauliflower into average pieces and put it into the blender.
2. Peel and slice the onion, and then put it into the blender as well.
3. Add eggs and semolina to the mixture.
4. Blend it fast until the received mass is homogeneous.
5. Take the mass out of the blender and complete it with flour, salt and chicken broth.
6. Mix the cauliflower dough.
7. Shape little balls from the mixture and put them into the Instant Pot.
8. Pour tomato juice onto them and shut the pressure cooker lid.
9. Turn on the "Steam" mode and let the meal cook for 20 minutes.
10. After the time has passed, turn of the Instant Pot and let the balls sit in it for 10 more minutes.
11. Take the meal out of the Instant Pot and put it into the plates.
12. Now you can enjoy the delicious dish!

Nutrition:
- Calories: 164
- Fat: 7g
- Carbohydrates: 17g
- Protein: 8g

Delectable Banana and Bread Porridge

This porridge of soft and creamy nature is adorable and does not require supplementary sugar. The dish is energizing yet does not contain excessive fat.

Prep time: 10 minutes
Cooking time: 15 minutes
Servings: 5

Ingredients:
- 3 bananas
- 1 cup of cream of your choice
- 1 cup of water
- 8 oz. of white bread
- 0.5 cup of walnuts
- 2 tablespoons of butter
- 0.5 teaspoon of salt

Directions:
1. Cut the white bread into small chunks and put them into the glass bowl.
2. Peel the 3 bananas and slice them finely.
3. Spread the banana pieces over the cut bread.
4. Grind the walnuts and cover the bread and banana with them.
5. Take a mixing dish and mix water with cream.
6. Blend this mixture thoroughly.
7. Cover the bread mixture with water and cream blend.
8. Add some butter and salt to the solution.
9. Place the glass bowl with the bread mixture into the pressure cooker.
10. Close the lid and turn on the "Porridge" mode.
11. Let the meal cook for 15 minutes.
12. Open the cooker's lid and stir the dish with the spoon.
13. The meal is finally ready to be served!
14. Serve it hot to secure its appetizing taste and flavor.

Nutrition:
- Calories: 433
- Fat: 21g
- Carbohydrates: 58g
- Protein: 9g

Spicy Sausages in Tomato Sauce

These sausages are good for health and nourishing. They will give you pleasure and an energy boost!

Prep time: 10 minutes
Cooking time: 8 minutes
Servings: 6

Ingredients:
- 3 eggs
- 1 sweet pepper
- 8 oz. of spicy chorizo sausages
- 0.3 cup of tomato juice
- 0.3 cup of fresh basil
- 0.3 cup of milk
- 1 tablespoon of flour
- 1 teaspoon of cilantro
- 1 teaspoon of olive oil
- 1 teaspoon of coriander
- 1 teaspoon of butter
- 0.25 teaspoon of thyme

Directions:
1. Take a bowl and put tomato juice, cilantro, flour, coriander, thyme and olive oil in it.
2. Blend this mixture with care.
3. Clear the sweet pepper from the seeds and cut it.
4. Wash the basil and cut it.
5. Pour milk into the tomato juice mixture and beat the eggs in.
6. Use a manual mixer to blend this solution until it is smooth with no clumps.
7. Add sliced pepper and butter into it.
8. Cut the sausages and place them into the mixture.
9. Put the mix into the pressure cooker and cook it for 6 minutes on the "Steam" mode.
10. Remove the lid and blend the mixture with a wooden spoon.
11. Shut the lid again and let the meal cook for 2 more minutes.
12. When the meal is ready, let it cool down for some time.
13. Serve it warm and enjoy it.

Nutrition:
- Calories: 198
- Fat: 13g
- Carbohydrates: 8g
- Protein: 13g

Fragrant Zucchini Pie

This light pastry meal is exquisite! Your family will love having it for breakfast and will ask for more.

Prep time: 15 minutes
Cooking time: 40 minutes
Servings: 6

Ingredients:
- 3 green zucchinis
- 2 onions
- 2 eggs
- 7 oz. of puff pastry
- 1 cup of dill
- 6 oz. of hard cheese
- 3 tablespoons of butter
- 0.5 cup of cream of your choice
- 1 teaspoon of paprika
- 1 teaspoon of salt

Directions:
1. Wash the zucchini and slice them.
2. Peel the onions and cut them into pieces.
3. Grate some hard cheese (you can use Cheddar).
4. Whip the eggs in a mixing dish.
5. Roll out the puff pastry.
6. Cover the basket of the Instant Pot with butter and put the rolled out dough inside.
7. Put sliced zucchini and cut onions on top of it.
8. Cover the mixture with paprika and salt.
9. Then cut the dill and add it to the mixture.
10. Cover the meal with the whipped eggs and grated cheese.
11. Complement the dish with cream.
12. Close the lid and turn on the "Steam" mode.
13. Let the meal cook for 40 minutes.
14. See if it is ready and take it out of the pressure cooker.
15. Let the meal chill for a short while and serve it!

Nutrition:
- Calories: 400
- Fat: 28g
- Carbohydrates: 26g
- Protein: 12g

Tortillas with Chicken and Vegetables

These special tortillas with meat and vegetables are the right beginning of your day! Taste them, and you will want to cook them again.

Prep time: 10 minutes
Cooking time: 45 minutes
Servings: 6

Ingredients:
- 1 pound of chicken
- 1 white onion
- 2 sweet peppers
- 8 oz. tortillas
- 1 cup of water
- 0.5 cup of chicken broth
- 0.5 cup of sweet corn
- 1 tablespoon of tomato paste
- 1 teaspoon of sour cream of your choice
- 1 teaspoon of ground black pepper
- 1 teaspoon of cilantro
- 0.5 teaspoon of turmeric
- 0.5 teaspoon of paprika

Directions:
1. Cut the chicken into slices and put it into your Instant Pot.
2. Cover it with chicken broth, water, sour cream and tomato paste.
3. Add ground black pepper, cilantro, turmeric and paprika to the mixture.
4. Clear the sweet peppers from the seeds, slice them, and peel the onion.
5. Spread sweet corn over the mixture and close the lid of the pressure cooker.
6. Switch on the "Steam" regime and let the meal cook for 30 minutes.
7. Open the lid, complete the meal with cut onion and sweet peppers.
8. Let the dish cook for 15 more minutes.
9. When it is ready, take the mixture out of the Instant Pot and fill the tortillas with it.
10. Wrap it and serve while warm.

Nutrition:
- Calories: 245
- Fat: 5g
- Carbohydrates: 30g
- Protein: 20g

Oatmeal with Pears and Raisins

This simple and low-fat meal is very easy to prepare. The taste of pears will make your oatmeal unforgettable!

Prep time: 5 minute
Cooking time: 6 minutes
Servings: 4

Ingredients:
- 2 cups of pear, cut and peeled
- 1 cup of water
- 1 cup of rolled oats
- 2 cups of milk
- 0.5 cup of raisins
- 0.5 cup of crushed walnuts
- 0.25 cup of brown sugar
- 1 tablespoon of butter
- 1 dash of salt
- 0.5 teaspoon of cinnamon dust

Directions:
1. Combine milk, oats, sugar, butter, raisins, pears, cinnamon, walnuts and salt in a bowl. Use a bowl that you can heat up in the Instant Pot.
2. Mix up all the ingredients mentioned above.
3. Put the bowl into the steamer basket of the Instant Pot.
4. Pour 1 cup of water into the pressure cooker.
5. Shut the lid and set the "High Pressure" mode.
6. Let the dish be prepared for 6 minutes.
7. Use a quick pressure release method when the porridge is ready.
8. Now you can put it into serving dishes and taste it.

Nutrition:
- Calories: 250
- Fat: 10g
- Carbohydrates: 14g
- Protein: 7g
- Fiber 11g

Luscious Fruit Cocktail

This fragrant fruit mixture will give you perfect mood in the morning! The beginning of your day will be much more pleasant because of it.

Prep time: 10 minutes
Cooking time: 15 minutes
Servings: 4

Ingredients:
- 1 sliced pear
- 1 sliced plum
- 1 sliced apple
- 3 tablespoons of coconut oil
- 2 tablespoons of honey
- 2 tablespoons of sunflower seeds
- 0.25 cup of ground coconut
- 0.25 cup of ground pecan nuts
- 0.5 teaspoon of ground cinnamon

Directions:
1. Place all the fruits into the bowl for cooking in Instant Pot.
2. Complete them with cinnamon, honey and coconut oil, and stir well.
3. Put the bowl into the steamer basket of the cooker.
4. Shut the basket and let the meal cook for 10 minutes.
5. Let the pressure to release, take out the dish and place the ingredients into a serving bowl.
6. Use the same heating bowl to mix up sunflower seeds with pecan nuts and coconut.
7. Put the bowl with the mixture in the pressure cooker.
8. Turn on the "Sauté" regime and let the mix prepare for 5 minutes.
9. Take it out and add it to the fruits you have cooked before.
10. Stir the mixture carefully and serve it.

Nutrition:
- Calories: 150
- Fat: 7g
- Carbohydrates: 12g
- Protein: 6g
- Fiber 3g

Oatmeal with Pomegranate Juice

The porridge has an amazing taste and plenty of vitamins. Be sure to try this recipe in the morning!

Prep time: 5 minutes
Cooking time: 2 minutes
Servings: 2

Ingredients:
- The seeds of 1 pomegranate
- 1 cup of porridge oats
- 1 cup of water
- 0.75 cup of pomegranate juice
- 1 dash of salt

Directions:
1. Place the porridge oats into the cooker.
2. Complement them with water, pomegranate juice and salt.
3. Blend the mixture and close the lid.
4. Let the porridge cook for 2 minutes at "High Pressure" mode.
5. When the time is up, make the pressure quick-release.
6. Open the lid, add the seeds of pomegranate to the porridge and stir it with a spoon.
7. Now the porridge is ready to serve.
8. Serve it and enjoy the delicious pomegranate flavor!

Nutrition:
- Calories: 200
- Fat: 3g
- Carbohydrates: 40g
- Protein: 7g

Baked Oats and Pumpkin

This health-giving dish will supply you with energy before the long day. Welcome it into your collection of recipes!

Prep time: 20 minutes
Cooking time: 13 minutes
Servings: 6

Ingredients:
- 1 cup of porridge oats
- 1 cup of pumpkin mash
- 3 cups of water
- 0.24 cup of maple syrup
- 2 tablespoons of cinnamon
- 1 tablespoon of butter
- 1 teaspoon of pumpkin pie spices
- 1 dash of salt

Directions:
1. Turn on your Instant Pot and set it to "Sauté" regime.
2. Put butter into the cooking bowl, let it melt and cover the bowl.
3. Place oats inside the bowl and then cook for 3 minutes.
4. Open the lid and complete the oats with pumpkin mash, water, salt, cinnamon, maple syrup and pumpkin pie spices.
5. Blend the mix, close the pressure cooker again and let the mixture prepare for 10 minutes at "High Pressure" mode.
6. Let the pressure release naturally (during 10 minutes) and stir the oats.
7. Cover them with the lid and let them sit for 10 more minutes.
8. The dish is now ready to be served!

Nutrition:
- Calories: 200
- Fat: 7g
- Carbohydrates: 33g
- Protein: 5g
- Sugar 14g

Browned-up Eggs with Spinach and Tomatoes

A healthy combination of greenery, vegetables and eggs is relevant in any season. Make it one of your favorite dishes!

Prep time: 10 minutes
Cooking time: 20 minutes
Servings: 6

Ingredients:
- 12 eggs
- 3 cups of fine cut spinach
- 1 cup of tomatoes, cut in cubes
- 1,5 cups of water
- 0.5 cup of milk
- 0.25 cup of grated hard cheese
- 3 green sliced onions
- 4 sliced tomatoes
- Black pepper and salt according to your preferences

Directions:
1. Fill your Instant Pot with the water.
2. Blend the eggs, pepper, salt, and milk in a bowl, stir them thoroughly.
3. Place cut tomatoes, green onions, and spinach in a baking bowl and blend them.
4. Cover the vegetables with the mixture of eggs, put the pieces of tomatoes on top of it, and spread hard grated cheese over the mix.
5. Put the mixture into the steamer basket of your pressure cooker, shut the lid and cook the dish for 20 minutes at "High Pressure" mode.
6. Release the pressure gradually, open the lid and replace the dish into the broiler, which has been preheated.
7. Keep the meal there until it has browned up slightly.
8. Now it is time to put the meal on the plates and serve it!

Nutrition:
- Calories: 200
- Fat: 10g
- Carbohydrates: 16g
- Protein: 10g

Delicious Eggs in Sausage Wrap

This is an original breakfast recipe, also known as Scottish eggs, is nourishing and tasty at the same time. Give it a shot!

Prep time: 10 minutes
Cooking time: 18 minutes
Servings: 4

Ingredients:
- 4 eggs
- 2 cups of water
- 1 pound of sausage mix of your choice
- 1 tablespoon of any vegetable oil

Directions:
1. Place the 4 unpeeled eggs into the Instant Pot and fill the cooker with 1 cup of water.
2. Close the lid and let the dish cook for 6 minutes at "High Pressure" mode.
3. Let the pressure release during 6 minutes.
4. Take out the eggs and put them into the dish filled with water and ice.
5. Now it is time to peel the eggs and set them aside.
6. Take the sausage mix and shape it into 4 balls.
7. Make them flat and put 1 egg on each piece of the mix.
8. Wrap the eggs in the mix and put them on a dish.
9. Switch on the "Sauté" regime of your Instant Pot, put some oil inside it and warm it up.
10. Put the eggs inside the pressure cooker, let them brown up on every side and put them back on the plate.
11. Fill the pressure cooker with the rest of the water.
12. Put the eggs into the steamer basket, close the lid and cook them at "High Pressure" mode for 6 minutes.
13. Use quick pressure release, put the eggs on serving dishes and enjoy them!

Nutrition:
- Calories: 300
- Fat: 21g
- Carbohydrates: 16g
- Protein: 12g

Light Eggs and Rice

This delightful airy dish will be ready very soon! Making it is a great chance to add diversity to your breakfast.

Prep time: 10 minutes
Cooking time: 5 minutes
Servings: 2

Ingredients:
- 2 eggs
- 1, 3 cups of water
- 1 dash of garlic dust
- 1 dash of sesame seeds
- 2 green onions, cut finely
- Salt and black pepper according to your taste
- Hot rice to serve with the eggs

Directions:
1. Take a mixing bowl, beat the eggs and mix them with 0.3 cup of water. Whip the eggs thoroughly.
2. Replace the mix into a heat-withstanding dish.
3. Complete the mix with sesame seeds, garlic dust, green onions, salt and pepper according to your taste. Whip the mix well.
4. Pour 1 cup of water into the pressure cooker.
5. Put the dish with the mix into the steamer basket of the Instant Pot.
6. Close the pot and let the dish cook at "High Pressure" mode for 5 minutes.
7. Let the pressure to release and open the lid.
8. Put the rice on serving plates and add egg mixture to it.
9. Enjoy the healthy meal!

Nutrition:
- Calories: 230
- Fat: 13g
- Protein: 21g
- Fiber 3g
- Sugar 1g

Gentle Oatmeal with Carrots and Maple Syrup

Prepare this useful dish and let it melt in your mouth! The combination of vegetables and oats is beneficial for your organism.

Prep time: 20 minutes
Cooking time: 13 minutes
Servings: 6

Ingredients:
- 4 cups of water
- 1 cup of chopped carrots
- 1 cup of porridge oats
- 0.25 cup of chia seeds
- 0.75 cup of raisins
- 3 tablespoons of maple syrup
- 1 tablespoon of butter
- 2 teaspoons of cinnamon
- 1 teaspoon of pie spices
- 1 dash of salt

Directions:
1. Turn on the "Sauté" mode.
2. Put some butter into the Instant Pot, let it heat up and melt.
3. Place the porridge oats into the Instant Pot, stir them and let them cook for 3 minutes.
4. Put ground carrots, maple syrup, water, spices, cinnamon and a dash of salt into the pot and blend them.
5. Close the lid and let the mixture cook at "High Pressure" regime for 10 minutes.
6. Let the pressure release naturally during 10 minutes.
7. Open the pressure cooker and complete the dish with chia seeds and raisins.
8. Stir the meal well and let it brew for 10 more minutes.
9. Spread it into serving dishes and have a wonderful breakfast!

Nutrition:
- Calories: 145
- Fat: 3g
- Carbohydrates: 25g
- Protein: 3.5g
- Sugar 11g

Stewed Rice with Cherries and Apple Juice

This dish is the embodiment of health and outstanding taste! Let yourself have it in the morning.

Prep time: 10 minutes
Cooking time: 12 minutes
Servings: 4

Ingredients:
- 2 apples
- 1 cup of apple juice
- 3 cups of milk
- 0.5 cup of dry cherries
- 0.3 cup of brown sugar
- 1,5 cups of short-grain rice (preferably Arborio)
- 1,5 teaspoons of cinnamon dust
- 2 tablespoons of butter
- 1 dash of salt

Directions:
1. Switch on your Instant Pot and set it to "Sauté" regime.
2. Put some butter inside the Instant Pot, heat it up and melt it.
3. Put the rice into the pressure cooker, stir it with a spoon and let the butter soak in.
4. Cook the rice for 5 minutes.
5. Cut out the core of the apples and slice them.
6. Put the chopped apples, apple juice, milk, cinnamon, salt and sugar into the Instant Pot.
7. Cover the pressure cooker with the lid and let the meal cook for 6 minutes. Use "High Pressure" mode.
8. Let the pressure release for 6 minutes.
9. Take off the lid, complete the dish with dried cherries, and blend them in.
10. Close the lid again and let the meal linger for 5 minutes more.
11. Fill the serving dishes and treat yourself to the meal!

Nutrition:
- Calories: 160
- Fat: 16g
- Carbohydrates: 30g
- Protein: 11g

Delicate Rice with Coconut Chips

The meal is light and simultaneously alimentative. Aromatic coconut milk will add beautiful flavor to your dish.

Prep time: 5 minutes
Cooking time: 7 minutes
Servings: 4

Ingredients:
- 1 cup of coconut milk
- 2 cups of water
- 1 cup of brown rice
- 0.5 cup of coconut chips
- 0.5 cup of maple syrup
- 0.25 cup of almonds
- 0.25 cup of raisins
- 1 dash of salt
- 1 dash of cinnamon dust

Directions:
1. Wash the rice, place it in a pot and cover it with water.
2. Cook it on the stove on average heat until it is ready.
3. Remove it to the Instant Pot upon readiness.
4. Complete it with coconut chips, milk, almonds, raisins, maple syrup, salt and cinnamon.
5. Blend the dish thoroughly and close the lid.
6. Let the meal prepare for 5 minutes under "High Pressure".
7. When it is done, select the quick pressure release method.
8. Now you can put the rice to serving dishes and enjoy it while it is warm.

Nutrition:
- Calories: 240
- Fat: 7g
- Carbohydrates: 45g
- Protein: 13g

Baked Rice with Mango

Soft rice topped with juicy mango is a refreshing morning dish. Let your family take pleasure in it!

Prep time: 10 minutes
Cooking time: 45 minutes
Servings: 4

Ingredients:
- 2 cups of black rice
- 2 sticks of cinnamon
- 5 pods of grated cardamom
- 3 pieces of clove
- 6.5 cups of water
- 0.75 cups of sugar
- 0.5 cup of grated coconut
- 1 dash of salt
- Sliced mango

Directions:
1. Wash the rice and dry it slightly.
2. Place it into the Instant Pot, cover it with water and add a dash of salt. Blend the mixture.
3. Mix cardamom with cinnamon and cloves, put it in cheesecloth and tie it.
4. Put it into the Instant Pot where the rice is and close the lid.
5. Cook the dish under "Low Pressure" during 35 minutes.
6. Let the pressure release naturally and open the lid.
7. Stir the rice with a spoon and complete it with coconut.
8. Turn on the "Sauté" mode and let the meal cook for 10 minutes more.
9. Take away the cloth with condiments and fill the serving dishes with the meal.
10. Put sliced mango on top of every serving.
11. The meal is ready!

Nutrition:
- Calories: 120
- Fat: 1g
- Carbohydrates: 21g
- Protein: 8g

Red Lentils with Fragrant Condiments

You will be happy with this meal once you try it! Make sure to let the lentils soak overnight so that they are succulent in the morning.

Prep time: 10 minutes
Cooking time: 30 minutes
Servings: 4

Ingredients:
- 1 cup of red lentils
- 3 cups of rooibos tea
- 2 sliced apples
- 1 teaspoon of ground turmeric
- 1 teaspoon of ground cloves
- 1 tablespoon of ground cinnamon
- Maple syrup according to your desire
- Coconut milk

Directions:
1. Soak the red lentils in the water during 4 hours and drain them.
2. Put them in your cooker.
3. Spread the tea on them and stir the mixture.
4. Close the lid and cook the dish under "High Pressure" for 15 minutes.
5. Upon releasing the pressure open the lid.
6. Complement the dish with apples, turmeric, cloves and cinnamon.
7. Stir it well, close the lid again and let the meal cook for 15 minutes. Use "High Pressure" mode as well.
8. Select the quick pressure release method and put the lentils into serving dishes.
9. Pour maple syrup and coconut milk on them according to your taste.
10. The dish is waiting to be tasted now!

Nutrition:
- Calories: 140
- Fat: 1.2g
- Carbohydrates: 35g
- Protein: 5g
- Sugar: 14g
- Fiber: 8g

Outstanding Millet Pie with Dates

This unusual meal will be highly appreciated by your family! Real gourmets will definitely take a pleasure in tasting it.

Prep time: 10 minutes
Cooking time: 10 minutes
Servings: 4

Ingredients:
- 7 oz. of water
- 14 oz. of coconut milk
- 0.6 cup of millet
- 4 pitted dates
- 1 dash of salt
- honey

Directions:
1. Spread the millet in the Instant Pot.
2. Complete it with dates, milk and a dash of salt.
3. Stir the mixture thoroughly.
4. Add some water to the mixture and blend it again.
5. Close the lid and let the meal cook for 10 minutes under "High Pressure".
6. Let the pressure release gradually and open the lid.
7. Serve the meal into dishes and cover it with as much honey as you desire.
8. The dish is prepared and ready to be tasted!

Nutrition:
- Calories: 240
- Fat: 20g
- Carbohydrates: 25g
- Protein: 8g
- Sugar 33g
- Fiber 2g

Delicate Boiled Millet with Cumin Seeds

This simple recipe is the right choice for your breakfast! Fill your morning with Asian notes.

Prep time: 10 minutes
Cooking time: 6 minutes
Servings: 4

Ingredients:
- 2 cups of organic millet
- 1 sliced white onion
- 3 cups of water
- 1 tablespoon of ghi
- 1 teaspoon of grated cardamom
- 3 teaspoons of the seeds of cumin
- 1 bay leaf
- Salt according to your taste
- Cinnamon stick (1 inch long)

Directions:
1. Turn on the "Sauté" regime of the Instant Pot.
2. Put ghi inside of it and let it warm up.
3. Fill the Pot with cinnamon, cumin, cardamom and bay leaf and stir all the condiments.
4. Let the spices cook for 1 minute.
5. Add sliced onion to the mixture and prepare it for 4 minutes.
6. Then complete the mix with millet, water and salt and stir it.
7. Close the lid and cook the meal under "High Pressure" for 1 minute.
8. Let the pressure release naturally and whip the mixture with a fork.
9. The dish is ready to be served.

Nutrition:
- Calories: 100
- Fat: 3g
- Carbohydrates: 16g
- Protein: 2.5g

Enjoyable Tapioca Pie

Baking this pie is a great way to treat your loved ones! It only takes a short time and brings a lot of pleasure.

Prep time: 5 minutes
Cooking time: 10 minutes
Servings: 4

Ingredients:
- 0.3 cup of tapioca balls
- 1.25 cups of whole milk
- 1.5 cups of water
- 0.5 cup of sugar
- Lemon zest (from one half of the lemon)

Directions:
1. Pour a cup of water into the Instant Pot.
2. Place tapioca balls into a heat withstanding bowl.
3. Cover them with 0.5 cup of water, milk, sugar and lemon zest.
4. Blend all the components and locate the bowl into the steamer basket of the Instant Pot.
5. Cover it with the lid and cook it for 10 minutes at "High Pressure" mode.
6. Let the pressure release naturally.
7. Put the baking into serving cups.
8. Treat your family with a nourishing meal!

Nutrition:
- Calories: 120
- Fat: 2g
- Carbohydrates: 21g
- Protein: 5g
- Sugar: 6g

Coconut and Chia Pie

The appetizing baking takes only 3 minutes to cook. You are welcome to taste it in the morning before a busy day!

Prep time: 2 minutes
Cooking time: 3 minutes
Servings: 4

Ingredients:
- 2 cups of almond milk
- 0.5 cup of chia seeds
- 0.25 cup of almonds
- 0.25 cup of grated coconut
- 4 teaspoons of sugar (or less, according to your taste)

Directions:
1. Place the chia seeds into the Instant Pot.
2. Cover them with milk, flaked coconut and almonds.
3. Stir the dish, close the lid and turn on the "High Pressure" mode.
4. Let the meal cook for 3 minutes.
5. Select the quick pressure release.
6. Put the pie into serving dishes and cover every piece with a teaspoon of sugar. Use as much sugar as you desire or as your diet permits.
7. The exquisite pie is ready to be served!

Nutrition:
- Calories: 130
- Fat: 12g
- Carbohydrates: 2g
- Protein: 14g

Yummy Hash and Veggies

The mix of potatoes and vegetables has an essential nutritional value. This meal will keep you going for a long time!

Prep time: 10 minutes
Cooking time: 8 minutes
Servings: 4

Ingredients:
- 1 package of frozen hash browns
- 8 oz. of ground sausage
- 1 sliced yellow onion
- 1 sliced sweet pepper
- 1 cup of grated hard cheese
- 0.3 cup of water
- 4 whipped eggs
- Salt and black pepper (according to your preferences)
- Salsa sauce

Directions:
1. Turn on the Instant Pot "Sauté" mode.
2. Put sausage inside it, blend it and prepare for 2 minutes.
3. Remove excessive fat.
4. Supplement the dish with sweet pepper and chopped onion, stir it and let it cook for 2 minutes.
5. Complete the meal with hash browns, eggs, water, grated cheese and salt.
6. Stir the mixture and let it prepare for 4 minutes. Use the "Low Pressure" mode.
7. When the dish is done, use the quick pressure release method.
8. Put the dish into plates and top it with salsa sauce if you want to make it more spicy.
9. Now the meal is prepared!

Nutrition:
- Calories: 300
- Fat: 16g
- Carbohydrates: 30g
- Protein: 17g

Crispy Fried Potatoes and Ham

This recipe is popular and always up-to-date. There are many ways to cook potatoes, and it is one of them!

Prep time: 10 minutes
Cooking time: 8 minutes
Servings: 4

Ingredients:
- 1 cup of grated hard cheese
- 6 whipped eggs
- 6 peeled and cut potatoes
- 1 cup of sliced ham
- 0.25 cup of water
- A drop of olive oil
- Salt and black pepper (according to your preferences)
- Toasted bread of your choice

Directions:
1. Switch on "Sauté" mode.
2. Drop just a little oil into the Instant Pot and warm it up.
3. Put cut potatoes inside, stir them and let them fry for 3 minutes.
4. Then complete the potatoes with sliced ham, whipped eggs, cheese, water, salt and pepper.
5. Stir this mix and close the lid.
6. Set the "High Pressure" regime and prepare the meal for 5 minutes.
7. When the pressure has been released naturally, put the fried potatoes into serving plates.
8. Add toasted bread to the servings and treat your family!

Nutrition:
- Calories: 250
- Fat: 12g
- Carbohydrates: 20g
- Protein: 17g

Tempting Berry Jam

It takes time to prepare this sweet dish, but it is worth it! Crusty bread pieces are delectable with jam on top of them.

Prep time: 20 minutes
Cooking time: 75 minutes
Servings: 12

Ingredients:
- 16 oz. of cut strawberries
- 16 oz. of cranberries
- 1 lemon (zest)
- 3 oz. of water
- 2.5 pounds of sugar
- 4 oz. of raisins
- 1 dash of salt
- Toasted bread

Directions:
1. Combine the berries, raisins and lemon zest in the Instant Pot.
2. Complete the mix with sugar, blend it with a spoon and let it sit in the pot for 1 hour.
3. When the time is up, pour the water into the mixture and add a dash of salt.
4. Close the lid and let the jam cook for 15 minutes. Use "High Pressure" mode.
5. When the pressure is released, let the jam linger for 5 more minutes.
6. Stir it and pour into little jars or bowls.
7. Put the pieces of toasted bread on plates and serve jam with them.

Nutrition:
- Calories: 60
- Fat: 0g
- Carbohydrates: 12g
- Protein: 1g
- Sugar: 12g

Amazing Lemon Jelly

The exotic homemade jelly is great with crispy bread and tea. It is a good substitute for jam if you do not feel like having it.

Prep time: 10 minutes
Cooking time: 14 minutes
Servings: 8

Ingredients:
- 2 pounds of lemons
- 4 pounds of sugar
- 1 tablespoon of vinegar

Directions:
1. Wash the lemons and cut them with a mandoline slicer.
2. Place the pieces of lemon into your Instant Pot.
3. Close the lid and let the fruit cook for 10 minutes under "High Pressure".
4. Let the pressure release when the time has passed.
5. Complete the jelly with sugar and vinegar, and close the pressure cooker again.
6. Cook the sweet dish for 4 more minutes. Use the "High Pressure" regime.
7. Let the pressure go down, blend the mass and pour it into formings or jars.
8. Keep the jelly in the fridge before you serve it.

Nutrition:
- Calories: 60
- Fat: 1g
- Carbohydrates: 12g
- Sugar: 13g

Unforgettable Sausage Ragout

This wholesome stew is a great example of solid breakfast. Try it and you will be satisfied!

Prep time: 10 minutes
Cooking time: 25 minutes
Servings: 5

Ingredients:
- 28 oz. of sliced tinned tomatoes
- 10 Italian sausages
- 15 oz. of your favorite tomato sauce
- 4 green sweet peppers, cut finely lengthwise
- 4 ground garlic cloves
- 1 cup of water
- 1 tablespoon of Italian dressing
- 1 tablespoon of dry basil

Directions:
1. Place the following ingredients into the Instant Pot: tomato sauce, tomatoes, basil, garlic, water, sweet peppers, sausages and Italian dressing.
2. Stir this mixture tenderly.
3. Close the lid of the Instant Pot and set the cooker to "High Pressure" mode.
4. Let the meal cook for 25 minutes.
5. Choose the quick pressure release way.
6. Now the dish is ready! It is time to serve it.

Nutrition:
- Calories: 400
- Fat: 31g
- Carbohydrates: 8g
- Protein: 23g

Enjoyable Blackberry Confiture

You have a chance to make a variety of jams with the help of Instant Pot. Here is the blackberry confiture option you might want to explore!

Prep time: 10 minutes
Cooking time: 23 minutes
Servings: 4

Ingredients:
- 5 cups of sugar
- Juice of 1 lemon
- 4 pints of fresh blackberries
- 3 tablespoons of pectin dust

Directions:
1. Place the fresh blackberries into the Instant Pot.
2. Combine them with the other components and blend carefully.
3. Choose the "Sauté" mode of the pressure cooker and let the solution cook for 3 minutes.
4. Relocate the confiture to the jars you have previously prepared. Make sure they are clean and dry.
5. Fill the jars with jam and put them into the steamer basket of the Instant Pot.
6. Add as much water as needed to cover one half of the jars' size.
7. Let the jars linger in a water bath for 20 minutes.
8. Then take the jars out and let them reach the room temperature.
9. It is best to keep your confiture in the fridge until the moment you offer it to your family in the morning.
10. If you put the confiture on bread and butter, the taste will be delicious!

Nutrition:
- Calories: 63
- Fat: 6g
- Carbohydrates: 12g
- Protein: 2g
- Sugar 7g

Roast-Beef Sandwiches with Soft Cheese

This energy-giving meal is a good nourishing breakfast. You can have the sandwiches at home and take them with you wherever you go.

Prep time: 10 minutes
Cooking time: 40 minutes
Servings: 8

Ingredients:
- 4 pounds of roast beef (finely sliced)
- 2 tablespoons of brown sugar
- 3 cups of beef broth
- 8 pieces of hard low-fat Italian cheese (Provolone)
- Salt and black pepper according to your taste
- 1 tablespoon of balsamic vinegar
- 2 tablespoons of Worcester sauce
- 4 tablespoons of butter
- 8 rolls for hoagie sandwiches
- 2.5 teaspoons of garlic dust
- 2 teaspoons of mustard powder
- 2 teaspoons of paprika
- 2 teaspoons of grated onion

Directions:
1. Place the roast beef into your Instant Pot.
2. Complete it with paprika, sugar, mustard and garlic powder, grated onion, broth, vinegar, Worcester sauce, and as much salt and pepper as you desire.
3. Stir the mixture carefully, close the Instant Pot and turn on "High Pressure" option.
4. Cook the dish for 40 minutes.
5. Let the pressure to quick release and remove the roast beef on the table to cut it.
6. Drain the liquid from the meat and leave it in a bowl.
7. Butter the sandwich rolls and slice the roast beef.
8. Put the meat on sandwich buns and add some cheese on top of it.
9. Place the buns into the broiler after it has been preheated and keep them there until the cheese melts.
10. Now you can soak the sandwiches with the sauce from the meat.
11. The dish is ready to be served!

Nutrition:
- Calories: 340
- Fat: 21g
- Carbohydrates: 12g
- Protein: 34g

Enticing Sappy Tacos

Those of you who love turkey meat will enjoy this dish. Fragrant condiments make it irresistible!

Prep time: 10 minutes
Cooking time: 5 minutes
Servings: 4

Ingredients:
- 1 tablespoon of Worcester sauce
- 1 tablespoon of extra-virgin olive oil
- 1.25 cups of beef broth
- 1 pound of sliced turkey meat
- 1 tablespoon of chili dust
- 2 teaspoons of corn flour
- 1.5 teaspoons of ground cumin
- 0.5 teaspoon of paprika
- 0.25 teaspoon of dry oregano
- 0.25 teaspoon of dry onions
- 0.25 teaspoon of garlic dust
- 0.25 teaspoon of onion powder
- 1 dash of spicy red pepper
- Salt and black pepper according to your preferences
- Taco shells

Directions:
1. Turn on the Instant Pot "Sauté" option.
2. Pour some oil inside and warm it up.
3. Put turkey meat and one half cup of broth into the pressure cooker and stir them.
4. Let the meat brown up for several minutes.
5. Get rid of excessive fat.
6. Complete the mixture with the remaining broth, Worcester sauce, flour, chili dust, cumin, garlic and onion powder, paprika, oregano, dry onions, red pepper, black pepper and salt. Blend this mix carefully.
7. Close the lid and switch on the "High Pressure" mode.
8. Let the dish cook for 5 minutes.
9. Afterwards let the pressure release naturally and open the lid.
10. Stir the mixture with a spoon and put it into Taco shells.
11. Now the meal can be served!

Nutrition:
- Calories: 240
- Fat: 11g
- Carbohydrates: 3.5g
- Protein: 31g

Gentle Grits with Cheese

The meal is traditional but does not lose its popularity. The grits are especially mellow and aromatic when cooked in the Instant Pot.

Prep time: 10 minutes
Cooking time: 13 minutes
Servings: 4

Ingredients:
- 1 cup of stone ground grits
- 3 cups of water
- 4 oz. of grated hard cheese
- 3 tablespoons of butter
- 2 tablespoons of coconut oil
- 2 teaspoons of salt
- Butter to top the servings

Directions:
1. Turn on the Instant Pot "Sauté" regime.
2. Put the grits into the pressure cooker and let them prepare for 3 minutes.
3. Complete them with coconut oil, water, butter, salt and grated cheese.
4. Stir the mixture, close the lid and set the Instant Pot to "High Pressure" regime.
5. Let the meal cook for 10 minutes.
6. Let the grits sit in the pressure cooker for 15 minutes while the pressure goes down.
7. Put them into serving dishes and place some butter on top.
8. You are welcome to taste the meal!

Nutrition:
- Calories: 280
- Fat: 13g
- Carbohydrates: 26g
- Protein: 13g
- Sugar 2g

Delicious Chickpeas Puree

This recipe gives you a new idea of how chickpeas puree can be made. Do not miss having it for breakfast!

Prep time: 5 minutes
Cooking time: 18 minutes
Servings: 8

Ingredients:
- 4 grated garlic cloves
- Juice of 1 lemon
- 6 cups of water
- 1 cup of soaked chickpeas
- 0.25 cup of cut parsley
- 1 bay leaf
- 2 tablespoons of tahini paste
- Salt according to your taste
- 1 dash of paprika
- 0.25 teaspoon of cumin
- Olive oil, extra-virgin

Directions:
1. Fill your Instant Pot with water and put chickpeas in it.
2. Complete them with 2 cloves of garlic and bay leaf.
3. Close the Instant Pot and turn on the "High Pressure" mode.
4. Let the meal cook for 18 minutes.
5. Let the pressure go down and pour out excessive liquid. Toss away the bay leaf. Leave some liquid for further steps.
6. Supplement the dish with tahini paste, the remaining cooking liquid, cumin, the juice of the lemon, the remaining garlic and some salt.
7. Mash the meal thoroughly to receive a nice puree.
8. Put the mass into serving dishes and top it with some olive oil and paprika.
9. It is time to enjoy the meal!

Nutrition:
- Calories: 270
- Fat: 19g
- Carbohydrates: 21g
- Protein: 7g

Nourishing Chicken Liver Blend

This meal is useful and will supply you with plenty of energy. Its unordinary components will add variety to your breakfast.

Prep time: 5 minutes
Cooking time: 15 minutes
Servings: 8

Ingredients:
- 0.75 pound of chicken liver
- 0.25 cup of red wine of your choice
- 1 yellow chopped onion
- 2 anchovies
- 1 tablespoon of butter
- 1 tablespoon of sliced capers
- 1 bay leaf
- 1 teaspoon of extra-virgin olive oil
- Black pepper and salt according to your taste

Directions:
1. Fill your Instant Pot with olive oil.
2. Put salt, pepper, chicken liver, onion, wine and bay leaf into it.
3. Mix the components, close the cooker and turn on the "High Pressure" mode.
4. Let the mixture cook for 10 minutes.
5. Let the pressure release quickly.
6. Complete the dish with anchovies, butter and capers.
7. Stir the meal and put it into the blender.
8. Make sure to blend it thoroughly.
9. Add some pepper and salt to the dish and blend it once again.
10. Now you can place it into breakfast bowls and serve with some toasted bread.

Nutrition:
- Calories: 150
- Fat: 12g
- Carbohydrates: 5g
- Protein: 4g

Zesty and Delicate Cheese Mass

This peppery cheese and sausage mass is a wonderful addition to your morning toasts! Top the toasts with this coating and enjoy them with a cup of tea or milk.

Prep time: 10 minutes
Cooking time: 5 minutes
Servings: 4

Ingredients:
- 4 cups of sliced whey cheese (preferably Ricotta)
- 10 oz. of cut tinned tomatoes and green chili peppers
- 1.75 cups of shredded Italian sausages
- 4 tablespoons of water

Directions:
1. Place the tomatoes, chili peppers, water, shredded sausages and cheese into your Instant Pot.
2. Mix the components, close the lid and set the pressure cooker to "High Pressure" mode.
3. Let the meal prepare for 5 minutes.
4. Let the pressure to release for 5 minutes.
5. Then open the lid, stir the mass and put it into serving bowls.
6. The meal is waiting for you to enjoy it!

Nutrition:
- Calories: 295
- Fat: 18g
- Carbohydrates: 4g
- Protein: 7g

Sweet Potatoes in the Enjoyable Sauce

If you are a potato-lover, you will definitely be satisfied with this meal. The sauce and pecan nuts are great supplements to the dish.

Prep time: 10 minutes
Cooking time: 15 minutes
Servings: 8

Ingredients:
- 1 cup of shredded pecan nuts
- 3 peeled and cut sweet potatoes
- 1 cup of water
- 0.5 cup of brown sugar
- 0.25 cup of butter
- 0.25 cup of maple syrup
- 1 tablespoon of corn flour
- 1 tablespoon of lemon peel
- 0.25 teaspoon of salt
- Whole pecans for serving

Directions:
1. Pour the water into the Instant Pot.
2. Supplement it with brown sugar, lemon peel and salt. Stir all the components.
3. Put the potatoes into the Instant Pot, close the lid and choose "High Pressure" regime.
4. Let the meal cook for 15 minutes.
5. Let the pressure go down and place the sweet potatoes to serving dishes.
6. Use your Instant Pot again. Turn on the "Sauté" mode, put butter into the Pot and let it melt.
7. Complete it with pecan nuts, maple syrup, and corn flour. Stir the mixture thoroughly.
8. Cover your sweet potatoes with this mixture.
9. Serve the potatoes covered in the sauce, with whole pecans on their side.
10. We hope that you will enjoy this meal!

Nutrition:
- Calories: 230
- Fat: 13g
- Carbohydrates: 15g
- Protein: 6g

Nectarous Pumpkin and Apple Spread

The honeyed coating is an original alternative to other kinds of spread. Use it on your toasted bread when you feel like sweetening up your morning.

Prep time: 15 minutes
Cooking time: 10 minutes
Servings: 18

Ingredients:
- 3 apples
- 30 oz. of pumpkin mash
- 1 cup of sugar
- 0.5 cup of honey of your choice
- 12 oz. of apple cider
- 1 tablespoon of pumpkin spices
- 1 dash of salt

Directions:
1. Peel the apples, take out their core and slice them.
2. Put pumpkin mash, pumpkin spices, apples, sugar, honey, cider and a dash of salt into the Instant Pot.
3. Blend the mixture well with a spoon.
4. Close the Instant Pot and turn on the "High Pressure" mode.
5. Let the dish cook for 10 minutes.
6. Let the pressure release for 15 minutes when the dish is done.
7. Place the mixture into little bowls and refrigerate it.
8. The meal can stay in the fridge for as long as several weeks. You can serve it any time.

Nutrition:
- Calories: 50
- Fat: 1g
- Carbohydrates: 10g
- Protein: 1g

Fragrant Puree with Legumes

This nourishing lunch will be of great benefit for you! The vegetable mix with legumes and spices is wonderful for your health.

Prep time: 10 minute
Cooking time: 30 minutes
Servings: 5

Ingredients:
- 2 white onions
- 4 cups of water
- 3 average size potatoes
- 2 cups of lentils
- 0.5 cup of fennel
- 0.5 tablespoon of ground black pepper
- 1 teaspoon of turmeric
- 1 teaspoon of cumin
- 1 teaspoon of cilantro
- 1 teaspoon of salt
- 0.5 teaspoon of oregano

Directions:
1. Put the lentils into the Instant Pot.
2. Cut the fennel and add it to the lentils.
3. Take a bowl and put cilantro, cumin, salt, oregano and ground black pepper into it. Blend the mix with care.
4. Peel and cut white onions.
5. Wash the tomatoes and slice them.
6. Put the sliced onions and tomatoes into the pressure cooker.
7. Cover the mixture with the spices you have blended in a bowl.
8. Add some water to the mix and blend it thoroughly.
9. Shut the lid and turn on the "Steam" mode.
10. Let the meal prepare for 30 minutes.
11. Let the dish cool down for a short while when it is ready.
12. Now you can put it into the serving plates and taste it!

Nutrition:
- Calories: 72
- Fat: 0.5g
- Cholesterol: 186mg
- Carbohydrates: 16g
- Protein: 4g

Chicken and Vegetables Salad

This salad is a valuable combination of warm poultry meat and greenery. It is an unquestionable source of vitamins!

Prep time: 15 minutes
Cooking time: 30 minutes
Servings: 6

Ingredients:
- 3 tomatoes of average size
- 2 cucumbers
- 3 oz. of black olives
- 5 oz. of Romaine lettuce
- 1 pound of chicken breast
- 0.5 lemon
- 1 tablespoon of olive oil
- 1 tablespoon of apple cider vinegar
- 1 teaspoon of salt
- 1 teaspoon of ground black pepper
- 1 teaspoon of basil
- 1 teaspoon of chili pepper

Directions:
1. Wash chicken breast and coat it with apple cider vinegar, salt, chili pepper and basil thoroughly.
2. Put chicken meat into the Instant Pot and shut the lid.
3. Turn on the "Poultry" regime of the pressure cooker and let the meal cook for half an hour.
4. While the meat is being prepared, cut the lettuce.
5. Afterwards slice the cucumbers, olives and tomatoes.
6. Put all these vegetables into a bowl and cover them with olive oil.
7. Press the juice out of the lemon half on top of the veggies.
8. After the meat is prepared, take it out of the Instant Pot and let it cool down a little bit.
9. Cut the chicken into average size slices.
10. Put this meat into the bowl where the vegetables are.
11. Use two wooden spoons to mix up the salad accurately.
12. The delicious salad is ready to be served right away!

Nutrition:
- Calories: 141
- Fat: 8g
- Carbohydrates: 9g
- Protein: 9g
- Fiber: 2g

Tender Soup with Chicken Legs and Carrots

This healthful soup will satisfy your appetite. You can serve it as it is or blend it and make it thicker.

Prep time: 10 minutes
Cooking time: 45 minutes
Servings: 8

Ingredients:
- 4 carrots
- 2 sweet peppers
- 2 white onions
- 5 cups of beef broth
- 0.5 cup of cream
- 1 pound of chicken legs
- 2 tablespoon of sour cream
- 1 teaspoon of paprika
- 1 teaspoon of salt

Directions:
1. Take the peel of the onions and slice them.
2. Peel the four carrots and shred them.
3. Put cream and beef broth into your Instant Pot.
4. Complete the broth with chicken legs and salt.
5. Shut the cooker's lid and turn on the "Poultry" regime.
6. Let the dish cook for 25 minutes.
7. Afterwards complement the meal with sliced onion, carrots and sour cream.
8. Clear the sweet peppers from the seeds and cut them thoroughly.
9. Put the peppers into the cooker and cover the dish with the lid.
10. Let the meal prepare for 20 minutes.
11. Take the dish out of the Instant Pot and spread some paprika over it.
12. The meal is ready to be served all at once!

Nutrition:
- Calories: 111
- Fat: 3.7g
- Carbohydrates: 16g
- Protein: 6g

Nourishing Cream Soup with Condiments

The dish has a great taste and value! Spicy garlic and seasoning give it the unforgettable flavor.

Prep time: 10 minutes
Cooking time: 35 minutes
Servings: 9

Ingredients:
- 1 cup of cream of your choice
- 4 cups of chicken broth
- 0.5 cup of milk
- 3 potatoes
- 1 pound of garlic cloves
- 1 tablespoon of butter
- 1 teaspoon of ground black pepper
- 1 teaspoon of oregano
- 1 teaspoon of basil
- 1 teaspoon of salt
- 0.5 teaspoon of lemon juice

Directions:
1. Clear the garlic cloves from the peel and cut them finely.
2. Combine the milk, cream, and chicken broth in the bowl.
3. Complete the liquid mixture with lemon juice, oregano, basil and ground black pepper.
4. Peel the potatoes and slice them.
5. Supplement the mixture with these potato slices.
6. Put the mix into the Instant Pot.
7. Put garlic and butter into the mixture.
8. Close the lid and turn on the "Soup" mode.
9. Let the meal cook for 35 minutes.
10. Check if all the components have prepared well. If so, take the bowl out of the Instant Pot and use the blender to mix the soup.
11. Make sure that the mixture is homogenous.
12. Pour the soup into the serving plates.

Nutrition:
- Calories: 282
- Fat: 8.5g
- Carbohydrates: 45g
- Protein: 10g

Health-giving Rice and Cabbage Rolls

Those of you who love kale will be fond of this dish! The enjoyable tomato sauce makes the rolls soft and even more pleasant to eat.

Prep time: 10 minutes
Cooking time: 25 minutes
Servings: 5

Ingredients:
- 1 cup of chicken broth
- 1 cup of cooked long grain rice
- 1 cup of beef broth
- 0.5 cup of tomato juice
- 0.25 cup of cream
- 1 pound of kale
- 1 yellow onion
- 1 egg
- 3 tablespoons of chives
- 1 tablespoon of curry
- 1 tablespoon of paprika
- 0.5 tablespoon of ground black pepper
- 1 teaspoon of olive oil
- 1 teaspoon of garlic dust
- 1 teaspoon of salt
- 1 teaspoon of oregano

Directions:
1. Put the prepared rice and curry into a bowl where you will mix the ingredients.
2. Beat the egg into this mixture.
3. Peel the onion and slice it finely.
4. Slice the chives as well and put these vegetables into a mixing bowl.
5. Complement the dish with oregano, paprika, salt, ground black pepper and garlic dust.
6. Blend the mixture manually with care until it becomes smooth.
7. Separate kale leaves, place some of the blend in the center of every leaf, and roll the leaves up.
8. Prepare the sauce for the rolls by joining chicken and beef broth, cream, tomato juice and olive oil. Stir the mix carefully.
9. Put the rolls into your Instant Pot and cover them with the sauce you have just prepared.
10. Close the lid and turn on the "Meat/Stew" regime. Let the meal cook for 25 minutes.
11. After the time has passed, open up the lid and let the meal cool down a little bit.
12. Remove the kale rolls to the plates and spread some tomato sauce on them.
13. You are welcome to enjoy the meal now!

Nutrition:
- Calories: 288
- Fat: 8g
- Carbohydrates: 45g

- Protein: 12g

Pungent Tomato Soup

This piquant vegetable soup is amazing for lunch. Add some of your favorite hard cheese to make it more delicious!

Prep time: 15 minutes
Cooking time: 35 minutes
Servings: 6

Ingredients:
- 4 cups of beef broth
- 0.3 cup of tomato paste
- 2 yellow onions
- 1 jalapeno pepper
- 1 pound of tomatoes
- 4 oz. of celery stems
- 5 oz. of hard cheese
- 1 bay leaf
- 2 tablespoons of sour cream
- 1 tablespoon of ground black pepper
- 0.5 tablespoons of ground chili pepper
- 1 teaspoon of thyme
- 1 teaspoon of coriander
- 1 teaspoon of cilantro
- 1 teaspoon of turmeric
- 1 teaspoon of salt

Directions:
1. Wash the tomatoes thoroughly, peel and slice them.
2. Put the condiments (coriander, cilantro, thyme, ground black pepper, ground chili, turmeric and salt) into the bowl for mixing.
3. Blend the spices carefully.
4. Pour the beef broth into the Instant Pot and add the sliced tomatoes.
5. Complete the broth with the mix of spices.
6. Clear the jalapeno pepper from the seeds and supplement the dish with it.
7. Complete the dish with bay leaf.
8. Close the lid and turn on the "Stew" regime. Let the meal cook for 15 minutes.
9. While the dish is being prepared, peel the onions, and slice them and celery stems.
10. When the 15 minutes have passed, add these vegetables into the Instant Pot.
11. Put some sour cream into the dish, shut the lid and cook the meal for 20 minutes more.
12. Grate the hard cheese of your choice while the meal is being cooked.
13. When the time is up, pour the soup into bowls. Spread some cheese on top.
14. Now the soup can be served!

Nutrition:
- Calories: 174
- Fat: 8g

- Carbohydrates: 17g
- Protein: 12g

Delicious Chicken and Yoghurt Mix

This mix of meat, fruits and yoghurt is wholesome and very tasty! Make sure to prepare it for lunch to have a chance to enjoy it!

Prep time: 15 minutes
Cooking time: 35 minutes
Servings: 6

Ingredients:
- 2 cups of water
- 1 cup of walnuts
- 0.5 cup of cranberries
- 0.5 cup of fresh dill
- 1 cup of plain yoghurt
- 3 apples
- 1 pound of chicken
- 3 tablespoons of lemon juice
- 1 teaspoon of cilantro
- 1 teaspoon of salt

Directions:
1. Spread salt on the chicken and put it into your Instant Pot.
2. Cover it with 2 cups of water and shut the lid.
3. Turn on the pressure cooker's "Poultry" mode.
4. Let the meal prepare for 35 minutes.
5. While the dish is being cooked, shred the walnuts thoroughly.
6. Slice the cranberries, take the peel off the apples and cut them as well.
7. Cover the apples with lemon juice to prevent them from turning dark.
8. Put the walnuts and berries into a mixing dish and stir them.
9. Cut the dill and add plain yoghurt to it. Use another dish.
10. Mix the blend until it becomes smooth, with no chunks.
11. Add cilantro to the blend and stir it again.
12. Upon readiness, take the chicken out of the Instant Pot and grate it.
13. Complete the mix of nuts and berries with the sliced chicken.
14. Cover the dish with the yoghurt blend.
15. Blend the mixture you have received with care to make sure it is consistent.
16. The chicken salad is ready to be served!

Nutrition:
- Calories: 257
- Fat: 12g
- Carbohydrates: 20g
- Protein: 19g

Cheese and Vegetable Pie

This fascinating creamy pie is a must-have for a lunch. We have no doubts that you will love it!

Prep time: 15 minutes
Cooking time: 25 minutes
Servings: 6

Ingredients:
- 2 cups of spinach
- 1 cup of cream
- 1 cup of green peas
- 8 oz. of hard cheese
- 2 onions
- 3 tablespoons of flour
- 1 teaspoon of salt
- 1 teaspoon of oregano
- 0.5 teaspoon of grated chili

Directions:
1. Wash the spinach and slice it, then put it into the mixing bowl.
2. Take the peel off the onions and slice them too.
3. Put salt, flour and grated chili into another bowl.
4. Supplement the mix with oregano and cream.
5. Whip the blend until it is homogenous.
6. Shred some hard cheese. You can use Parmesan, for example.
7. Put the green peas into the Instant Pot and cover them slightly with shredded cheese.
8. Add some sliced onion to the peas and cover the meal with another layer of shredded cheese.
9. Cover this mixture with sliced spinach and top it with the rest of the cheese.
10. Add the blended cream mix to this dish and close the lid.
11. Turn on the "Steam" mode and let the meal prepare for 25 minutes.
12. When the time is up, let the dish cool down a little bit.
13. Replace it into serving plates and enjoy it!

Nutrition:
- Calories: 270
- Fat: 10g
- Carbohydrates: 27g
- Protein: 20g

Red Beans and Chili Sauté

This enticing sauté is very nutrient! Try it once and you will want to cook it again.

Prep time: 10 minutes
Cooking time: 37 minutes
Servings: 6

Ingredients:
- 2 sweet peppers
- 1 can of red beans
- 2 cups of beef broth
- 2 cups of lentils
- 1 cup of chicken, sliced thoroughly
- 0.5 cup of corn
- 1 tablespoon of ground chili
- 1 tablespoon of sour cream of your choice
- 1 tablespoon of tomato paste
- 0.5 tablespoon of garlic dust
- 1 teaspoon of salt
- 1 teaspoon of cumin
- 1 teaspoon of shredded onion

Directions:
1. Put ground chili, lentils, canned red beans and corn into the Instant Pot.
2. Complete the mix with beef broth and turn on the "Sauté" regime.
3. Let the mix prepare for 7 minutes and stir it with a spoon.
4. When the time has passed, cover the dish with salt, shredded onion, garlic dust, ground chicken and cumin.
5. Free the sweet peppers from the seeds and slice them.
6. Add the sweet peppers to the mix.
7. Supplement the mix with some tomato paste.
8. Shut the lid and turn on the "Bean/Chili" mode for 30 minutes.
9. Check if the dish is cooked well and stir it with the wooden spoon many times.
10. If you find that the meal is prepared, take it out of the pressure cooker.
11. The delicious lunch is ready to be served hot and tasted!

Nutrition:
- Calories: 212
- Fat: 5g
- Carbohydrates: 32g
- Protein: 15g

Succulent Pork Chops

This recipe is widely known and we are sure that you will find it appetizing as well!

Prep time: 10 minutes
Cooking time: 16 minutes
Servings: 6

Ingredients:
- 1 pound of pork chops
- 2 eggs
- 0.5 cup of flour
- 0.25 cup of milk
- 1 teaspoon of cilantro
- 1 teaspoon of lemon juice
- 1 teaspoon of ground black pepper
- 1 teaspoon of turmeric
- 1 teaspoon of salt

Directions:
1. Beat the pork chops thoroughly.
2. Make a mixture of turmeric, salt, cilantro and ground black pepper.
3. Stir all the components and rub the condiments into the pork chops.
4. Drop some lemon juice on the pork and set the meat aside for about 10 minutes to soak in the juice.
5. While the meat is being marinated, beat the eggs into the mixing bowl and whip them with a manual mixer. Add some milk to the eggs.
6. Stir the mixture and dip the meat slices into it.
7. Cover the pork slices with flour.
8. Pour a little olive oil into the Instant Pot and turn on the "Sauté" mode to preheat it.
9. Then put the pork chops into the pressure cooker and prepare them for 8 minutes on every side, using the same mode.
10. When the meal is ready, let it cool off slightly and serve it soon!

Nutrition:
- Calories: 250
- Fat: 12g
- Carbohydrates: 10g
- Protein: 24g

Tasteful Corn Soup

This gentle soup is easy to make and it will bring you much health! It is refreshing and implies the necessary vitamins.

Prep time: 10 minutes
Cooking time: 35 minutes
Servings: 9

Ingredients:
- 5 cups of chicken broth
- 2 cups of fresh corn
- 1 cup of cream
- 3 potatoes of average size
- 2 white onions
- 2 cloves of garlic
- 0.5 cup of fresh cilantro
- 1 teaspoon of salt
- 1 teaspoon of coriander
- 1 teaspoon of chili pepper

Directions:
1. Place the chicken broth and cream into your Instant Pot.
2. Clear the onions and garlic cloves from the peel and slice them.
3. Peel the potatoes and cut them into pieces.
4. Put the sliced onions, potatoes and garlic into the Instant Pot.
5. Cover the mixture with coriander and salt.
6. Close the lid and turn on the "Soup" regime.
7. Let the meal prepare for 20 minutes.
8. Slice the fresh cilantro and add the corn.
9. Complete the soup with this mix and stir it with a wooden spoon thoroughly.
10. Close the lid and let the meal cook for 15 minutes more. Use the same mode as before.
11. After the dish is prepared, let it sit for 10 minutes.
12. Now the meal can be served!

Nutrition:
- Calories: 364
- Fat: 9g
- Carbohydrates: 60g
- Protein: 11g

Luscious Lasagna with Beef

This stewed lasagna is a great choice for a family picnic! It will give you energy and unforgettable pleasure.

Prep time: 15 minutes
Cooking time: 35 minutes
Servings: 6

Ingredients:
- 1 cup of tomato juice
- 1 cup of ground beef
- 0.5 cup of cream cheese
- 0.5 cup of chicken broth
- 1 white onion
- 10 oz. of hard cheese
- 9 oz. lasagna noodles
- 1 teaspoon of sour cream of your choice
- 1 teaspoon of ground black pepper
- 1 teaspoon of cilantro
- 1 tablespoon of butter
- 0.5 teaspoon of salt

Directions:
1. Put the sour cream, tomato juice, chicken broth and salt into a mixing dish.
2. Blend the mix with a spoon carefully.
3. Shred some hard cheese and take off the onion peel.
4. Grate the onion thoroughly.
5. Take another bowl and put ground beef, ground black pepper and cilantro into it.
6. Stir the mix with care.
7. Put a piece of butter into the pressure cooker and top it with the ground beef mixture.
8. Turn on the "Stew" regime and let the mix cook for about 10 minutes.
9. Do not forget to stir it often.
10. Take the mixture out of the Instant Pot.
11. Put lasagna noodles into the pot and cover them with tomato juice.
12. Top this mix with the chopped onion, shredded cheese and the ground beef mixture.
13. Keep on making the layers until all the components have been used up.
14. Close the lid and turn on the "Manual" regime. Let the meal prepare for 25 minutes.
15. Let the dish cool off when it is ready and feel free to serve it afterwards!

Nutrition:
- Calories: 450
- Fat: 28
- Carbohydrates: 20g
- Protein: 28

Homemade Cottage Cheese with Almonds

This unusual meal is wonderful both for breakfast and lunch! It is light and can be completed with fruits or jam of your choice.

Prep time: 5 minutes
Cooking time: 28 minutes
Servings: 5

Ingredients:
- 6 cups of milk
- 0.3 cup of almonds
- 0.3 cup of sour cream of your choice
- 0.25 cup of apple cider vinegar
- 3 tablespoons of honey
- 1 teaspoon of salt

Directions:
1. Put the milk into the Instant Pot and close the lid.
2. Turn on the "Yogurt" regime of the pressure cooker and let the milk heat up until it boils. Keep the lid open when doing it.
3. Whip the milk when it is heating up and add 1 teaspoon of salt.
4. Keep adding the vinegar in portions when the milk is being prepared. Do not forget to stir it.
5. Close the lid and unplug the pressure cooker.
6. Let the milk sit in it for 25 minutes.
7. Take a sieve and cover it with cheesecloth.
8. Toss yoghurt on it and let it excrete the whey completely.
9. Put the dish into the blender and blend it thoroughly.
10. Complete the mixture with sour cream and honey to sweeten it up.
11. Blend it for 3 more minutes.
12. Put the cheese into serving plates and cover it with the almonds you have ready.
13. Delicate cottage cheese can be tasted now!

Nutrition:
- Calories: 245
- Fat: 11g
- Carbohydrates: 27g
- Protein: 10g

Spicy Tacos with Pork

Those of you who love Mexican food will appreciate this dish! Corn tortillas go with this filling very well.

Prep time: 10 minutes
Cooking time: 35 minutes
Servings: 6

Ingredients:
- 2 cups of chicken broth
- 0.5 cup of spinach
- 0.5 cup of cilantro
- 1 pound of shredded pork
- 1 tablespoon of salt
- 1 tablespoon of olive oil
- 1 tablespoon of tomato paste
- 1 tablespoon of onion dust
- 1 teaspoon of oregano
- 1 teaspoon of cumin
- 1 teaspoon of ground black pepper
- 1 teaspoon of red hot chili pepper
- 0.5 teaspoon of shredded coriander

Directions:
1. Prepare the spinach and cilantro by washing and slicing them.
2. Put the mix of this greenery into the mixing dish.
3. Complete it with shredded pork and cover the mix with salt, cumin and oregano.
4. Blend the mixture carefully.
5. Put it into the Instant Pot and add olive oil.
6. Turn on the "Sauté" regime and let it cook for 10 minutes.
7. Remember to stir the mix often.
8. Supplement the mix with ground black pepper, onion dust and tomato paste.
9. Complete it with chicken broth and blend it.
10. Prepare the mix in the Instant Pot at "Stew" regime for 25 minutes.
11. Let the taco filling cool down a little bit.
12. Then put it on top of tortillas and serve the dish.

Nutrition:
- Calories: 286
- Fat: 19g
- Carbohydrates: 5.5g
- Protein: 22g

Savory Tortilla Rolls

This lunch meal is quick to make and truly delightful. If you like ham, tomatoes and condiments, this is the dish for you!

Prep time: 10 minutes
Cooking time: 8 minutes
Servings: 5

Ingredients:
- 8 oz. of ham
- 6 oz. of tomatoes
- 1 red onion
- 5 corn tortillas
- 0.5 cup of lettuce
- 0.25 cup of tomato paste
- 3 tablespoons of lemon juice
- 1 teaspoon of oregano
- 1 teaspoon of salt
- 1 teaspoon of ground black pepper

Directions:
1. Wash the lettuce and slice it.
2. Cut the ham into pieces.
3. Wash the tomatoes and onions and slice them as well.
4. Mix salt, ground black pepper and oregano in a mixing bowl. Stir the blend.
5. Cover the tortillas with tomato paste.
6. Spread chopped lettuce, onions, tomatoes and ham onto them.
7. Cover them with the mix of condiments and pour lemon juice on them.
8. Wrap the tortillas according to your taste and put them into the Instant Pot.
9. Turn on the "Manual" mode for 8 minutes.
10. Once the time is up, take the rolls out of the pressure cooker and serve them hot.

Nutrition:
- Calories: 140
- Fat: 2g
- Carbohydrates: 21g
- Protein: 11g

Delectable Pepperoni Pizza

This familiar dish is very easy to make in the Instant Pot. Hot and fragrant pizza will be welcomed by your loved ones!

Prep time: 15 minutes
Cooking time: 35 minutes
Servings: 8

Ingredients:
- 8 oz. of yeast dough
- 6 oz. of pepperoni
- 5 oz. of hard cheese (preferably Cheddar)
- 4 oz. of black olives
- 1 egg
- 0.5 cup of tomatoes
- 3 tablespoons of tomato paste
- 2 tablespoons of basil
- 1 tablespoon of sour cream
- 1 tablespoon of fresh cilantro
- 1 teaspoon of olive oil
- 1 teaspoon of oregano

Directions:
1. Use the rolling pin to roll out the dough and form a circle.
2. Cover the Instant Pot with olive oil on the inside and put the pizza base in there.
3. Mix the tomato paste and sour cream.
4. Cover the base of pizza with this mixture.
5. Cut the pepperoni and black olives into pieces.
6. Spread these pieces on pizza.
7. Grate some cheese and slice the cilantro.
8. Cover pizza with the cilantro.
9. Cut the tomatoes into pieces and put them on top of pizza.
10. Cover pizza with grated cheese.
11. Supplement it with basil and oregano.
12. Top the pizza with shredded cheese and close the lid.
13. Turn on the "Manual" regime and let the dish prepare for 35 minutes.
14. After that time let the pizza stay in the Instant Pot with the open lid for a short while.
15. Put it into serving dishes and cut it according to the number of portions.

Nutrition:
- Calories: 230
- Fat: 14g
- Carbohydrates: 10g
- Protein: 16g

Aromatic Italian Pie

This nutrient pie with cheese and ham will give your lunch an Italian spirit. It is so crisp and delicious, that you will not be able to resist it!

Prep time: 10 minutes
Cooking time: 35 minutes
Servings: 4

Ingredients:
- 8 oz. of ham
- 7 oz. of hard cheese of your choice
- 6 oz. of yeast dough
- 1 cup of whey cheese (Ricotta)
- 1 tablespoon of butter
- 1 teaspoon of lemon juice
- 1 teaspoon of paprika

Directions:
1. Use the rolling pin to roll out the dough, giving it a round shape.
2. Shred the cheese and slice the ham.
3. Cover one half of the dough circle with shredded cheese and sliced ham.
4. Put whey cheese on top of that.
5. Cover the mix with paprika and wrap the pie to make it crescentic.
6. Put a piece of butter into the pressure cooker and let it melt.
7. Put the pie into the Instant Pot and pour some lemon juice on it.
8. Close the lid and turn on the pressure cooker's "Manual" mode.
9. Let the meal prepare for 35 minutes.
10. Flip the pie to another side to let it brown up there as well. Do it one time while the meal is being cooked.
11. Once the dish is ready, take it out of the Instant Pot.
12. The luscious pie can be put on a serving dish.

Nutrition:
- Calories: 490
- Fat: 26g
- Carbohydrates: 22g
- Protein: 42g

Nutrient Chicken Sandwiches

This recipe is an ideal variant of fast and tasty lunch. Hot sandwiches can be prepared every day!

Prep time: 10 minutes
Cooking time: 4 minutes
Servings: 6

Ingredients:
- 5 oz. of hard cheese (Cheddar, for example)
- 8 oz. of smoked chicken
- 5 oz. of sandwich bread of your choice
- 1 pitted avocado
- 0.25 cup of sunflower sprouts
- 3 tablespoons of garlic sauce
- 2 tablespoons of lemon juice
- 1 tablespoon of mustard
- 1 teaspoon of sesame seeds
- 1 teaspoon of onion dust
- 1 teaspoon of butter

Directions:
1. Cut the sandwich bread into 6 pieces.
2. Mix the lemon juice, garlic sauce, onion dust and mustard. Blend the mixture thoroughly.
3. Cover each piece of bread with the mustard mix.
4. Cut the Cheddar cheese and avocado.
5. Slice the smoked chicken.
6. Cover 3 pieces of bread with the cut cheese, avocado, and slices of smoked chicken.
7. Spread some sesame seeds on the mixture.
8. Cover the pieces of bread with the remaining bread slices to form sandwiches.
9. Put some butter into the cooker.
10. Place the sandwiches into the Instant Pot and turn on the "Sauté" regime.
11. Let the dish cook for 2 minutes, flip the sandwiches and let them cook for 2 minutes more.
12. Now you can relocate your lunch to serving plates and cut the sandwiches in halves.
13. The meal is ready to be served!

Nutrition:
- Calories: 360
- Fat: 28g
- Carbohydrates: 12g
- Protein: 16g

Flavorful Chicken Burritos

These aromatic rolls will suit those of you who are fond of chipotle and tomato paste. It is a wholesome and energizing meal.

Prep time: 10 minutes
Cooking time: 35 minutes
Servings: 5

Ingredients:
- 2 cups of water
- 0.3 cup of fresh parsley
- 0.25 cup of salsa
- 1 pound of chicken
- 3 oz. of lettuce
- 5 corn tortillas
- 3 tablespoons of chipotle paste
- 1 tablespoon of tomato paste
- 1 tablespoon of garlic dust
- 1 teaspoon of chili pepper
- 1 teaspoon of mayo sauce
- 1.2 teaspoon of cayenne pepper

Directions:
1. Slice the chicken into average pieces and put it into your Instant Pot.
2. Complete it with cayenne pepper, chili pepper and garlic powder.
3. Add the water to the dish and close the lid.
4. Turn on the "Poultry" regime and let the meat cook for half an hour.
5. While it is being cooked, tear the lettuce into pieces and put it into the mixing bowl.
6. Supplement it with mayo sauce and salsa and stir the mix.
7. Put salsa and chipotle paste on the tortillas.
8. Slice the parsley finely and spread it on tortillas evenly.
9. Cover them with lettuce mixture and tomato paste.
10. Cut the chicken finely when it is prepared and put the meat slices on the tortillas.
11. Roll the tortillas and put them into the Instant Pot.
12. Switch on the "Stew" regime and set the time for 5 minutes.
13. When the meal is ready, take it out of the pressure cooker and serve it.

Nutrition:
- Calories: 180
- Fat: 3g
- Carbohydrates: 16g
- Protein: 21g

Refreshing Cabbage Stew

To make this dish more colorful you can use various types of cabbage. It is a healthy and exquisite lunch!

Prep time: 10 minutes
Cooking time: 45 minutes
Servings: 6

Ingredients:
- 1 pound of cabbage
- 1 onion
- 2 carrots
- 5 eggs
- 0.5 cup of tomato juice
- 0.5 cup of bread crumbs
- 1 tablespoon of butter
- 0.5 tablespoon of flour
- 1 teaspoon of salt
- 1 teaspoon of paprika
- 1 teaspoon of cilantro

Directions:
1. Cut the cabbage and spread some salt on it.
2. Blend it and let it sit aside until it marinates well and gives juice.
3. Put tomato juice and cilantro into the mixing bowl and blend them.
4. Place some butter into the Instant Pot and let it melt.
5. Put sliced cabbage into the Instant Pot and turn on the "Sauté" regime.
6. Let cabbage cook for 10 minutes. Remember to stir it often.
7. Beat the eggs into the bowl and whip them.
8. Add flour to them and blend the mass until it is homogenous.
9. Put the tomato mix into the Instant Pot and stir it thoroughly.
10. Top it with the egg mixture and bread crumbs.
11. Cover the dish with paprika.
12. Peel and slice the onion and carrots.
13. Add them to the Instant Pot and stir the mix.
14. Shut the lid and turn on the "Manual" option. Let the meal cook for 35 minutes.
15. After the dish is prepared, let it cool off and serve it.

Nutrition:
- Calories: 180
- Fat: 10g
- Carbohydrates: 13g
- Protein: 10g

Enjoyable Egg and Vegetable Wraps

These wraps have a splendid taste and are nutrimental. If you make them you will get 2 meals in 1 – egg pancakes and vegetable wraps.

Prep time: 10 minutes
Cooking time: 15 minutes
Servings: 6

Ingredients:
- 6 corn tortillas
- 7 oz. of beetroot
- 4 eggs
- 1 carrot of average size
- 1 red onion
- 1 cup of lettuce
- 4 tablespoons of salsa
- 1 tablespoon of lemon juice
- 1 tablespoon of olive oil
- 1 teaspoon of salt
- 1 teaspoon of cilantro
- 1 teaspoon of lemon zest
- 0.5 teaspoon of ground black pepper
- 0.5 teaspoon of paprika

Directions:
1. Beat the eggs into the bowl for mixing and whip them.
2. Complete the eggs with salt, ground black pepper, cilantro and paprika.
3. Stir the mixture with a spoon thoroughly.
4. Use some cooking spray to cover the inner side of the Instant Pot.
5. Turn on the "Sauté" regime and place the egg mix into the pressure cooker to prepare a pancake.
6. Flip it to another side in 1 minute and let it cook for 1 minute more.
7. Do the same to make 5 more egg pancakes.
8. Let them cool down.
9. Cover the tortillas with salsa, lemon juice and lettuce.
10. Put egg pancakes on top of the tortillas.
11. Cut the carrots finely, slice the onion and beetroot.
12. Put vegetables on top of tortillas, cover them with lemon zest and wrap the tortillas.
13. Place the wraps into the pressure cooker and turn on the "Manual" mode.
14. Let the meal cook for 3 minutes.
15. Take the dish out of the pressure cooker and serve it while it is hot.

Nutrition:
- Calories: 190
- Fat: 9.5g
- Carbohydrates: 19g
- Protein: 9g

Onion and Carrot Soup

This is the example of a light and pleasant lunch meal. It can be served immediately or prepared beforehand.

Prep time: 15 minutes
Cooking time: 25 minutes
Servings: 6

Ingredients:
- 1 cup of cream
- 4 cups of beef broth
- 1 pound of yellow onions
- 2 oz. of unsalted butter
- 1 average size carrot
- 1 teaspoon of salt
- 1 teaspoon of turmeric
- 1 teaspoon of ground black pepper
- 1 teaspoon of cilantro
- 0.5 teaspoon of white pepper
- 0.5 teaspoon of nutmeg

Directions:
1. Clear the onions and carrot from the peel and grate them.
2. Mix the vegetables with each other and add salt, black and white pepper, turmeric, nutmeg and cilantro to the mixture. Blend it well.
3. Put some butter into the Instant Pot and wait until it melts down.
4. Place the onion and carrot mix into the pressure cooker and turn on the "Sauté" mode.
5. Let the vegetables brown up for about 10 minutes. Do not forget to stir them when they are being cooked.
6. Complete the mixture with cream and beef broth and stir it.
7. Turn on the "Meat/Stew" mode and cook the mix for 15 minutes with the closed lid.
8. Afterwards take the dish out of the pressure cooker and let it cool down for a short while.
9. Now you can fill the bowls with the meal and serve it!

Nutrition:
- Calories: 277
- Fat: 24g
- Carbohydrates: 11.5g
- Protein: 5g

Seasoned Potato Dumplings

It does not take a long time to prepare this dough product. It has a savory taste and is nutritive.

Prep time: 10 minutes
Cooking time: 20 minutes
Servings: 4

Ingredients:
- 8 oz. of ground potatoes
- 4 cups of water
- 0.5 cup of flour
- 1 teaspoon of salt
- 1 teaspoon of oregano
- 1 teaspoon of paprika
- 0.5 teaspoon of white pepper

Directions:
1. Put the ground potatoes into the Instant Pot.
2. Cover the vegetable with flour, water, salt, oregano, paprika and white pepper.
3. Blend the mix with a spoon and close the lid.
4. Turn on the "Manual" mode and prepare the meal for 10 minutes.
5. Mix the dish again and take it out of the Instant Pot.
6. Knead the dough manually and shape little balls out of it.
7. Fill the Instant Pot with the 3 cups of water and let it preheat.
8. Put the balls into warm water and stir them.
9. Close the lid and turn on the "Steam" mode.
10. Let the meal prepare for up to 10 minutes (the time depends on when the dumplings are ready).
11. Take the meal out of the Instant Pot and put it on serving dishes.
12. Let it cool off and cover it with the sauce or topping according to your taste.
13. Feel free to serve the delicious dumplings!

Nutrition:
- Calories: 115
- Fat: 3g
- Carbohydrates: 18g
- Protein: 3g

Fried Chickpea Balls

Zesty falafel is the traditional food of the Middle East. You can use either canned or pre-cooked chickpeas to make this lovely dish.

Prep time: 15 minutes
Cooking time: 10 minutes
Servings: 6

Ingredients:
- 3 garlic cloves
- 4 oz. of shallots
- 1 cup of prepared chickpeas
- 0.5 cup of olive oil
- 0.5 cup of parsley
- 3 tablespoons of tahini paste
- 1 tablespoon of sesame seeds
- 1 tablespoon of lemon juice
- 2 teaspoons of water
- 1 teaspoon of cumin
- 1 teaspoon of salt
- 1 teaspoon of paprika
- 1 teaspoon of ground chili
- 1 teaspoon of garlic dust
- 0.5 teaspoon of coriander
- 0.5 teaspoon of sea salt

Directions:
1. Use the blender to mix up the chickpeas, coriander, cumin, salt, parsley, paprika, ground chili, garlic dust and water.
2. Blend all the components until the mass is homogenous.
3. Cut the cloves of garlic and shallot.
4. Complete the chickpeas mix with sliced shallot.
5. Keep on blending the mix for 1 more minute.
6. Take a mixing dish and mix up the sesame seeds and sea salt. Stir the mix well.
7. Shape average size balls from the chickpeas mixture and cover them with the sesame mix.
8. Pour some olive oil into the Instant Pot and turn on the "Sauté" regime. Let the oil boil.
9. Place the balls you have prepared into boiling oil and let them cook for about 1 minute. Keep them in the oil until you can see the crust.
10. Put the balls into paper towels and get rid of unnecessary oil.
11. Mix up the sliced garlic, lemon juice and tahini paste.
12. Whip the mix until the mass is smooth.
13. Cover the prepared balls with the tahini sauce.

Nutrition:
- Calories: 362
- Fat: 25g
- Carbohydrates: 28g

- Protein: 9g

Exotic Salad with Beef and Halloumi Cheese

This delicate salad will suit both the meat and vegetable lovers. Orange juice and arugula give it an incomparable taste.

Prep time: 15 minutes
Cooking time: 10 minutes
Servings: 6

Ingredients:
- 7 oz. of Halloumi cheese
- 1 pound of beef tenderloins
- 1 cup of Romaine lettuce
- 0.5 cup of arugula
- 1 tablespoon of lemon juice
- 1 tablespoon of orange juice
- 1 tablespoon of olive oil
- 1 teaspoon of rosemary
- 1 teaspoon of ground white pepper
- 1 teaspoon of salt
- 1 teaspoon of apple cider vinegar
- 1 teaspoon of sesame oil
- 0.5 teaspoon of cumin

Directions:
1. Beat the beef tenderloins thoroughly.
2. Cover them with lemon juice, apple cider vinegar, ground white pepper, salt, rosemary and cumin.
3. Make sure the meat is well coated and let it marinate for a while.
4. Put it into the Instant Pot and turn on the "Sauté" regime.
5. Let the meat cook for 10 minutes or more, depending on readiness.
6. Remember to turn it over to another side once in a while.
7. When the meat is ready, slice it into fine pieces and put them into the serving dish.
8. Tear the Romaine lettuce and complete the meat pieces with it.
9. Cut the Halloumi cheese and coat it in sesame oil.
10. Slice the arugula and add all the components to the salad.
11. Pour some orange juice on the mixture and blend it with a spoon.
12. The salad is ready to be served!

Nutrition:
- Calories: 289
- Fat: 16g
- Carbohydrates: 4.5g
- Protein: 29g

Thick Soup with Mushrooms and Cream

This soup has a very pleasant texture and taste. It is especially good for those who enjoy mushrooms!

Prep time: 20 minutes
Cooking time: 37 minutes
Servings: 6

Ingredients:
- 6 cups of chicken broth
- 1 cup of rich milk (or milk and cream mixture)
- 0.25 cup of garlic
- 9 oz. of cremini mushrooms
- 5 oz. of shallot
- 3 oz. of potatoes
- 2 oz. of celery
- 1 teaspoon of fresh thyme leaves
- 1 teaspoon of butter
- 1 teaspoon of salt

Directions:
1. Clear the peel off the garlic cloves and cut them.
2. Shred the cremini mushrooms and mix them with cut garlic.
3. Put the mix into the Instant Pot and cover it with butter.
4. Turn on the "Sauté" regime for 7 minutes. Stir the mix often.
5. Peel the potatoes and slice them.
6. Complete the mushroom mixture with potatoes.
7. Cut the shallot and celery and put them into the Instant Pot as well.
8. Cover the mix with salt, milk and cream mixture, and chicken broth.
9. Slice the thyme leaves, add them to the mix and stir it.
10. Close the lid and turn on the "Soup" mode.
11. Let the dish prepare for half an hour.
12. Afterwards turn off the Instant Pot and use a manual mixer to blend the dish.
13. Make sure the soup becomes thick like a cream.
14. Pour the soup into serving bowls and enjoy the taste!

Nutrition:
- Calories: 279
- Fat: 4.5g
- Carbohydrates: 52g
- Protein: 12g

Beef and Rice Sauté

This dish is especially yummy when served hot. Feel free to use your favorite type of meat!

Prep time: 15 minutes
Cooking time: 26 minutes
Servings: 4

Ingredients:
- 2 cups of ground beef
- 3 cups of water
- 1 cup of long grain rice
- 0.25 cup of tomato paste
- 0.25 cup of soy sauce
- 1 tablespoon of lemon juice
- 1 tablespoon of olive oil
- 1 tablespoon of ground black pepper
- 1 tablespoon of cilantro
- 1 teaspoon of cut garlic
- 1 teaspoon of salt

Directions:
1. Put the ground beef into the Instant Pot.
2. Complete it with cilantro, salt, ground black pepper and cut garlic.
3. Add olive oil to the mix and blend it with care.
4. Turn on the "Sauté" regime for 6 minutes.
5. Use a spoon to stir the mix thoroughly.
6. Complete the mass with rice and stir it again.
7. Supplement the dish with tomato paste, lemon juice and water.
8. Stir the mix and close the lid.
9. Turn on the "Rice" regime and let the meal prepare for 20 minutes.
10. Upon readiness, cover the dish with soy sauce and blend it with a spoon.
11. Now the meal is ready to be served!

Nutrition:
- Calories: 440
- Fat: 19g
- Carbohydrates: 44g
- Protein: 23g

Chicken Breasts in Apricot Sauce

This meal is breathtaking and alimentative. It will rapidly fill you with energy! You can use steamed rice to come with it as garnish.

Prep time: 10 minutes
Cooking time: 12 minutes
Servings: 6

Ingredients:
- 6 chicken breasts without skin and bones
- 16 oz. of canned apricots
- 16 oz. of Russian salad dressing
- 0.25 cup of water
- 1 package of onion soup mixture
- 0.25 teaspoon of dried oregano
- 0.25 teaspoon of cayenne pepper
- ground black pepper
- salt

Directions:
1. Use some salt and pepper to cover the chicken breasts.
2. Rub some dried oregano and cayenne pepper into them.
3. Whip the onion soup mixture, Russian salad dressing and canned apricots in one bowl and prepare a sauce.
4. Put the chicken meat into the Instant Pot and pour the sauce over it.
5. Shut the lid and turn on the "High Pressure" regime for 6 minutes.
6. Let the pressure release naturally during 12 minutes.
7. Take out the chicken meat, drain it and let it sit aside for a while.
8. Switch on the "Sauté" mode and let the sauce boil a little until it becomes thicker.
9. Pour the sauce on top of chicken breasts or by their side and serve the meal!
10. If you want your meat to be more savory, you are welcome to add a dash of cinnamon or nutmeg dust to canned apricots.

Nutrition:
- Calories: 293
- Fat: 10.9g
- Carbohydrates: 20.5g
- Protein: 28.3g

Stewed Chicken in Salsa

Coat the chicken with condiments and lime juice and let it soak before cooking. Your whole family will enjoy this dish!

Prep time: 10 minutes
Cooking time: 6 minutes
Servings: 4

Ingredients:
- 2 pounds of chicken breasts
- 2 cups of fresh tomato salsa
- 3 tablespoons of lime juice
- 1 teaspoon of sea salt
- 1 teaspoon of cumin
- 0.5 teaspoon of ground black pepper

Directions:
1. Take a mixing bowl and blend the salt, ground black pepper and cumin.
2. Rub the mixture into chicken meat.
3. Put the chicken breasts into the Instant Pot and cover them with tomato salsa.
4. Close the lid and let the meal cook under "High Pressure" for 6 minutes.
5. Let the pressure release naturally.
6. Take the chicken meat out of the sauce, grate it and put it back into the Instant Pot.
7. Stir the sauce thoroughly and serve it.

Nutrition:
- Calories: 183
- Fat: 3.5g
- Carbohydrates: 8.6g
- Protein: 29g

Instant Homemade Hot Dogs

This traditional meal can be made at home very quickly! The hot dogs are aromatic and will make a fabulous lunch.

Prep time: 5 minutes
Cooking time: 3 minutes
Servings: 6

Ingredients:
- 6 hot dogs including the casing
- 6 hot dog buns
- 1 quart of water
- 1 tablespoon of white wine vinegar
- 0.5 teaspoon of cumin
- 0.125 teaspoon of nutmeg dust

Directions:
1. Put the water, vinegar, cumin and nutmeg dust into the Instant Pot and stir them.
2. Place the hot dogs into the pressure cooker and close the lid.
3. Let them prepare under "Low Pressure" for 3 minutes.
4. Afterwards let the pressure release naturally.
5. Take out the hot dogs and let them dry.
6. Put the hot dogs into buns and cover them with the dressing of your choice. You can use ketchup, mustard or fried beans for the delicious taste.

Nutrition:
- Calories: 454
- Fat: 22.5g
- Carbohydrates: 48.3g
- Protein: 13.8g

Flavorsome Adobo Carnitas

You should definitely try this pungent and aromatic dish! You will love the soft meat and fragrant condiments.

Prep time: 15 minute
Cooking time: 60 minutes
Servings: 4

Ingredients:
- 2.5 pounds of pork roast, cut into fine pieces
- 3/4 cup of chicken broth
- 2 or 3 chipotle adobo peppers in adobo sauce
- 4 cloves of cut garlic
- 2 bay leaves
- 1 tablespoon of vegetable oil
- 2 teaspoons of salt
- 1.5 teaspoons of cumin
- 0.5 teaspoon of adobo condiments
- 0.5 teaspoon of garlic dust
- 0.25 teaspoon of dried oregano
- black pepper
- salt

Directions:
1. Cover the pork with some pepper and salt.
2. Warm up the oil in a big pan, and put the roast in it for about 5 minutes to let it brown up.
3. Make little cuts in the pieces of pork roast and place some garlic into every cut.
4. Put the roast and the rest of the ingredients into the Instant Pot.
5. Close the lid and cook them under "High Pressure" for 50 minutes.
6. After that time let the pressure be released naturally.
7. Take out the pork roast pieces, drain them and cut into thin slices.
8. You can serve the dish in tortillas or taco shells.
9. If you would like to add more flavor to the meal, you can top it with tomato salsa or guacamole.

Nutrition:
- Calories: 851
- Fat: 46.2g
- Carbohydrates: 8.8g
- Protein: 96g
- Fiber 3.1g

Cream Soup with Italian Sausages

This refreshing dish can be supplemented with red hot chili pepper and can be served with garlic bread. This special garnish will emphasize the divine taste!

Prep time: 10 minutes
Cooking time: 15 minutes
Servings: 6

Ingredients:
- 1 pound of Italian sausages
- 3 large sliced potatoes
- 1 yellow onion, sliced finely
- 1.5 quarts of chicken broth
- 2 cups of chopped kale
- 1 cup of rich cream
- 0.25 cup of water
- 4 pieces of sliced bacon
- 2 grated garlic cloves
- salt
- ground black pepper

Directions:
1. Turn on the "Sauté" regime of the Instant Pot and heat it up.
2. Put the bacon inside the Instant Pot, let it brown up and become crispy, then take it out.
3. Place sliced onion into the pressure cooker and cook it at "Sauté" mode for 3 minutes.
4. Add Italian sausages to the dish and cook them for 5 more minutes.
5. Complete the dish with garlic and let it cook for 1 more minute.
6. Supplement the meal with water, chicken broth, potatoes, salt and pepper.
7. Close the lid and let the dish cook under "High Pressure" for 5 minutes.
8. Let the pressure release on its own.
9. Turn on the "Sauté" regime again, put kale into the Instant Pot, and let the meal boil until the kale softens.
10. Add cream and the condiments of your taste to the soup.
11. Use crispy bacon as garnish and serve the soup warm.

Nutrition:
- Calories: 1179
- Fat: 74.5g
- Carbohydrates: 95.1g
- Protein: 38.2g
- Fiber 13.4g

Tender Rice Porridge

You can use any kind of meat with this delicate porridge. This luscious meal will keep you going for a long time!

Prep time: 10 minutes
Cooking time: 40 minutes
Servings: 6

Ingredients:
- 5 cups of water
- 2 cups of rice
- 1 pound of chicken fillet
- 1 tablespoon of oregano
- 1 tablespoon of butter
- 0.5 cup of fresh dill
- 1 teaspoon of salt
- 1 teaspoon of turmeric
- 1 teaspoon of rosemary
- 0.5 teaspoon of ground ginger

Directions:
1. Mix the rice and water and put them into the Instant Pot.
2. Complete the dish with ground ginger and oregano.
3. Slice the chicken fillet and put it into the Instant Pot too.
4. Blend the mix and close the lid.
5. Cook the meal for 30 minutes under "High Pressure".
6. Supplement the dish with butter, turmeric, dill and rosemary.
7. Stir the mix thoroughly.
8. Turn on the "Sauté" regime of the pressure cooker for 10 more minutes.
9. When the time is up, take the porridge out of the pressure cooker and let it cool down.
10. The dish is ready to be served in the bowls.

Nutrition:
- Calories: 344
- Fat: 21g
- Carbohydrates: 37g
- Protein: 14g

Delicate Potatoes and Rice

This dish will be even better if you add some butter to it. Enjoy it with your whole family!

Prep time: 25 minutes
Cooking time: 13 minutes
Servings: 4

Ingredients:
- 1 cup of rice
- 4 cups of chicken broth
- 1 red onion
- 8 oz. of potatoes
- 2 tablespoons of olive oil
- 1 tablespoon of tomato paste
- 0.5 tablespoon of paprika
- 1 teaspoon of turmeric
- 1 teaspoon of salt
- 1 teaspoon of cilantro
- 1 teaspoon of basil
- 0.5 teaspoon of coriander

Directions:
1. Take the peel off the onion, slice it and put it into the Instant Pot.
2. Cover it with olive oil, rice and salt.
3. Turn on the "Sauté" mode for 3 minutes.
4. Remember to stir the mix often so that it does not burn.
5. Peel the potatoes, cut them and add them to the mixture. Blend the mass.
6. Complete it with chicken broth, paprika, turmeric, cilantro, basil, tomato paste and coriander.
7. Blend the mix with care using a wooden spoon.
8. Cook the dish under "High Pressure" for 10 minutes with the lid closed.
9. When the time has passed, take the meal out of the pressure cooker.
10. Let the rice meal sit aside for 15 minutes and put it into the plates.
11. Now you can enjoy the dish!

Nutrition:
- Calories: 302
- Fat: 16g
- Carbohydrates: 37g
- Protein: 12g

Pleasant Lentil Stew

This mixture of legumes and vegetables is very good for your health! We guarantee that you will be satisfied with it.

Prep time: 15 minutes
Cooking time: 30 minutes
Servings: 6

Ingredients:
- 5 cups of beef broth
- 2 cups of lentils
- 0.25 cup of thyme leaves
- 2 carrots
- 0.5 lemon
- 1 tablespoon of sour cream of your choice
- 1 tablespoon of ground black pepper
- 1 teaspoon of salt
- 0.5 teaspoon of sugar

Directions:
1. Peel the carrots and slice them.
2. Cut the lemon into pieces.
3. Put the salt, sugar, sour cream and ground black pepper into the bowl for mixing.
4. Grate the leaves of thyme and complete the mix with them.
5. Put the lentils into your Instant Pot.
6. Supplement them with lemon and beef broth.
7. Add the mixture of condiments, as well as the carrots, to the dish and stir it thoroughly until the mix is homogenous.
8. Close the lid and let the meal cook for 30 minutes under "High Pressure".
9. When the meal is prepared, blend it with a wooden spoon.
10. Put the meal into serving plates and spread some salt over it, if you wish.
11. The dish can be served and enjoyed!

Nutrition:
- Calories: 71
- Fat: 0.6g
- Carbohydrates: 12g
- Protein: 7g

Juicy Pasta with Beef and Tomato Sauce

This Italian pasta will be the adornment of your lunch. Make sure to try it! You can add some grated cheese on top of pasta.

Prep time: 10 minutes
Cooking time: 14 minutes
Servings: 6

Ingredients:
- 8 oz. of penne pasta
- 4 cups of chicken broth
- 1 cup of shredded beef
- 0.5 cup of tomato sauce
- 2 white onions
- 3 tablespoons of chives
- 2 tablespoons of soy sauce
- 0.5 tablespoon of paprika
- 1 teaspoon of turmeric
- 1 teaspoon of cilantro
- 1 teaspoon of olive oil
- 1 teaspoon of salt

Directions:
1. Peel and cut the onions, and put them into the Instant Pot.
2. Cover them with turmeric, salt, cilantro, and paprika.
3. Blend the mix thoroughly and turn on the "Sauté" mode.
4. Let the meal cook for 4 minutes. Remember to stir it.
5. Complete it with tomato sauce, soy sauce, and chives.
6. Let it cook at "Sauté" regime for 3 more minutes.
7. Supplement the dish with penne pasta and chicken broth.
8. Add the shredded beef to the dish and close the lid.
9. Prepare the meal for 7 minutes under "High Pressure".
10. Let the pressure release naturally and open the lid afterwards.
11. Mix pasta with care and place it onto serving dishes.

Nutrition:
- Calories: 245
- Fat: 10g
- Carbohydrates: 22g
- Protein: 15g

Soft Vegetable Squash with Meat

This exquisite airy meal will leave nobody impartial! Do not miss a chance to have it on your table.

Prep time: 10 minutes
Cooking time: 20 minutes
Servings: 6

Ingredients:
- 2 cups of water
- 1 cup of shredded beef
- 0.3 cup of tomato paste
- 15 oz. of vegetable spaghetti
- 1 tablespoon of paprika
- 1 teaspoon of thyme
- 1 teaspoon of your favorite sour cream
- 1 teaspoon of salt

Directions:
1. Put shredded beef, salt, paprika, tomato paste, sour cream and thyme into the bowl for mixing.
2. Blend the mix until it is smooth.
3. Put the blend into the Instant Pot.
4. Turn on the "Meat/Stew" regime and let the dish prepare for 10 minutes. Keep stirring it.
5. Take the mixture out of the pressure cooker.
6. Pour some water into the Instant Pot.
7. Slice the vegetable spaghetti into 4 pieces and put it into the steamer.
8. Close the lid and let the vegetable prepare under "High Pressure" for 10 minutes.
9. Afterwards let it cool down a little bit.
10. Squish the vegetable with the fork and add shredded beef mixture to it.
11. Mix the meal and serve it while it is warm.

Nutrition:
- Calories: 109
- Fat: 5.5g
- Protein: 9g
- Carbohydrates: 7g
- Fiber 2g

Fragrant Soup with Beef Brisket and Cheese

This soft and tender soup is nourishing and delightful. Make sure to serve it hot!

Prep time: 15 minutes
Cooking time: 40 minutes
Servings: 8

Ingredients:
- 10 oz. of beef brisket
- 8 oz. of broccoli
- 10 oz. of hard cheese
- 7 cups of water
- 1 cup of green beans
- 0.5 cup of parsley
- 0.25 cup of coriander leaves
- 1 carrot
- 1 tablespoon of sour cream
- 1 teaspoon of salt
- 1 teaspoon of cilantro
- 1 teaspoon of ground black pepper
- 1 teaspoon of lemon juice

Directions:
1. Put the beef brisket, broccoli, green beans and salt into the Instant Pot.
2. Clear the carrot from the peel and slice it.
3. Put the sliced carrot into the Instant Pot and pour the water in it.
4. Close the lid and let the meal cook under "High Pressure" for 30 minutes.
5. Take the cooker's vessel out carefully to avoid burning yourself.
6. Take out the beef brisket and blend the remaining mix until it is homogenous.
7. Put the pressure cooker's vessel into the Instant Pot again.
8. Complete the dish with sour cream, ground black pepper, cilantro and lemon juice.
9. Slice the parsley and the leaves of coriander and complete the dish with them.
10. Shred some hard cheese, spread it over the mixture and let the meal cook for 10 more minutes.
11. By the time the dish is cooked the cheese should have melted.
12. Blend the meal thoroughly until it is nice and smooth.
13. Take the dish out of the pressure cooker and complete it with beef brisket.
14. Replace the soup into serving dishes and taste it!

Nutrition:
- Calories: 152
- Fat: 9g
- Carbohydrates: 7g
- Protein: 311g

Red Beans and Quinoa Salad

The taste of this exotic meal is fascinating! You can serve it either warm or cooled, if you prepare it beforehand.

Prep time: 10 minutes
Cooking time: 20 minutes
Servings: 6

Ingredients:
- 2 cups of chicken broth
- 1 cup of quinoa
- 1 can of red beans
- 2 cucumbers
- 5 tomatoes
- 1 yellow onion
- 2 tablespoons of tomato paste
- 1 teaspoon of salt
- 1 teaspoon of olive oil
- 1 teaspoon of sour cream

Directions:
1. Put the quinoa into your Instant Pot.
2. Complete it with chicken broth and canned red beans.
3. Blend the mix and cover it with the lid.
4. Let the meal prepare under "High Pressure" for 20 minutes.
5. Take the mix out of the pressure cooker and let it cool down.
6. Cut the cucumbers, onion and tomatoes.
7. Put all the vegetables together into the bowl for mixing.
8. Complete the mix with sour cream, tomato paste and olive oil.
9. Blend the mix with care and complete it with quinoa and beans blend.
10. Spread some salt over the dish and mix the salad until the dish is smooth.
11. The meal is ready to be served!

Nutrition:
- Calories: 230
- Fat: 4g
- Carbohydrates: 37g
- Protein: 11g

Crispy Sandwiches with Egg Mayonnaise

This meal is truly festive because of its style and taste. It is very suitable for the lunch outside or as a party snack.

Prep time: 5 minutes
Cooking time: 10 minutes
Servings: 2

Ingredients:
- 2 brown baguettes
- 6 big eggs
- 6 tablespoons of rich mayonnaise
- 1 big carrot
- 0.9 oz. cucumber
- 0.9 oz. of spring onions
- 0.9 oz. hard cheese
- 1 teaspoon of mustard dust
- 1 teaspoon of parsley
- butter
- salt and pepper

Directions:
1. Pour 0.7 cup of water on the bottom of your Instant Pot.
2. Put the eggs on the steam rack inside the pressure cooker.
3. Cover the Instant Pot with the lid and close it securely. Turn on the "Steam" regime for 5 minutes.
4. Meanwhile peel and cut the carrot finely. Wash and slice the cucumber and spring onions, and shred the cheese.
5. Place all these components except the onion into a bowl. Fill the bowl with condiments, complete it with mayonnaise and blend thoroughly. Cut the baguettes in halves.
6. When the eggs are ready, you will hear the beeping. Move the valve to open the lid and let the steam out.
7. Take the eggs out, put them into cold water and peel them.
8. Now remove the eggs to the mixing bowl with other components and mash them with a fork. Keep mashing until the mass is smooth.
9. Free the steamer from the water and turn on the "Sauté" regime for 5 minutes. Cover the slices of bread with butter and put them into the pressure cooker so that the butter faces downwards. Continue doing this until the butter melts and the bread browns up. It should take 2 to 3 minutes.
10. Take the baguettes out and put the spring onions in their place. Cook the onions at the same mode until they have stewed well.
11. Cover the flavorful baguettes with the stewed onions, egg mayonnaise and the fresh greenery of your choice.
12. The amazing sandwiches are ready to be served!

Nutrition:
- Calories: 611
- Fat: 37.1g
- Carbohydrates: 53.3g

- Protein: 27.3g

Cream Salad with Pasta

This salad is gentle, but rich and nourishing at the same time. You will enjoy the mix of pasta, bacon and your favorite vegetables.

Prep time: 10 minutes
Cooking time: 20 minutes
Servings: 6

Ingredients:
- 3 cups of chicken broth
- 0.5 cup of bread crumbs
- 0.5 cup of lettuce
- 0.5 cup of cream
- 5 oz. of fried bacon
- 5 oz. of hard salty cheese (preferably Romano)
- 5 oz. of pasta
- 0.5 lemon
- 2 tomatoes
- 3 tablespoons of mayonnaise
- 1 teaspoon of basil
- 1 teaspoon of paprika

Directions:
1. Put pasta and chicken broth into the Instant Pot.
2. Complete the dish with paprika and basil and blend the mix.
3. Close the lid and turn on the "High Pressure" mode for 20 minutes.
4. While the dish is being cooked, tear the lettuce and put it into the plate for mixing.
5. Squeeze some lemon juice over the lettuce so that the juice covers the vegetable.
6. Mix mayonnaise and cream and blend the mixture with care.
7. Slice some Romano cheese and fried bacon.
8. Cut the tomatoes into fine pieces.
9. When the pasta is ready, take it out of the pressure cooker and wash it with hot water a little bit.
10. Complete the lettuce mix with pasta, sliced tomatoes, cheese and fried bacon.
11. Spread some cream mixture and bread crumbs over the dish.
12. Blend the mixture thoroughly and put it into serving dishes.

Nutrition:
- Calories: 320
- Fat: 21g
- Carbohydrates: 18g
- Protein: 15g

Delicate Soup with Miso Paste

Preparing this dish will bring variety to your lunch meals. The traditional Japanese paste will give exotic flavor to your soup.

Prep time: 8 minutes
Cooking time: 10 minutes
Servings: 6

Ingredients:
- 5 cups of chicken broth
- 0.5 cup of soy sauce
- 5 oz. of celery stems
- 1 white onion
- 1 tablespoon of miso paste
- 1 tablespoon of sesame seeds
- 0.5 tablespoon of shredded ginger
- 1 teaspoon of turmeric
- 1 teaspoon of cilantro
- 1 teaspoon of salt
- 1 teaspoon of lemon zest

Directions:
1. Put the shredded ginger, cilantro, turmeric, salt, lemon zest and chicken broth into the Instant Pot.
2. Peel the onion, slice it and the celery stems as well. Place the vegetables into the Instant Pot.
3. Blend the mixture and close the lid.
4. Turn on "High Pressure" mode for 8 minutes.
5. Complete the dish with miso paste and soy sauce.
6. Blend the mix thoroughly until the miso paste has melted.
7. Prepare the meal for 2 more minutes and pour the soup into serving dishes.
8. Taste the refreshing meal!

Nutrition:
- Calories: 155
- Fat: 7g
- Carbohydrates: 14g
- Protein: 7g
- Fiber: 1g

Aromatic Salad with Tuna and Vegetables

This dish is far from being ordinary! Your family members will take pleasure in tasting it.

Prep time: 15 minutes
Cooking time: 20 minutes
Servings: 6

Ingredients:
- 1 pound of tuna
- 2 red onions
- 2 bell peppers of your choice
- 5 oz. of tomatoes
- 1 cup of lettuce
- 0.5 cup of water
- 0.3 cup of pecan nuts
- 0.25 cup of cream of your choice
- 2 tablespoons of lemon juice
- 2 tablespoons of butter
- 1 teaspoon of olive oil
- 1 teaspoon of salt
- 0.5 teaspoon of rosemary

Directions:
1. Cover the tuna with salt and rosemary and blend it tenderly.
2. Put the butter into the Instant Pot and add the tuna.
3. Pour some water into the pressure cooker and close the lid.
4. Turn on the "High Pressure" mode and prepare the meal for 20 minutes.
5. While the dish is being cooked, peel and slice the onions.
6. Cut the lettuce, tomatoes and bell peppers.
7. Crack the pecan nuts.
8. Combine the lemon juice, olive oil and cream in the mixing plate and blend the mix with care.
9. Fill the mixing dish with all the vegetables and mix them tenderly.
10. When tuna is ready, take it out of the pressure cooker and slice it.
11. Add sliced tuna to the vegetable mix.
12. Blend the salad with two spoons for your convenience.
13. Fill the serving bowls with the salad and drop some cream sauce on it.
14. It is not necessary to stir the salad any longer. Just start enjoying it!

Nutrition:
- Calories: 190
- Fat: 11g
- Carbohydrates: 7g
- Protein: 17g
- Fiber 2g

Homemade Bread with Cheese

It is amazing that you can bake bread at home now, isn't it? Enjoy this cheesy soft baguette while it is warm.

Prep time: 15 minutes
Cooking time: 30 minutes
Servings: 6

Ingredients:
- 2 eggs
- 8 oz. of Mozzarella cheese
- 5 oz. of Parmesan cheese
- 2 cups of flour
- 1 cup of fresh spinach
- 0.3 cup of whey
- 1 tablespoon of sugar
- 1 tablespoon of rosemary
- 1 tablespoon of butter
- 1 teaspoon of yeast
- 1 teaspoon of salt
- 1 teaspoon of parsley
- 1 teaspoon of cilantro
- 1 teaspoon of oregano

Directions:
1. Mix the whey and the yeast, and blend the mixture until the yeast has diffused within the liquid.
2. Complete the mix with sugar, salt and cilantro, and stir it.
3. Add flour to the mix and knead the homogenous dough.
4. Cut the parsley and combine it with oregano, rosemary, butter and eggs.
5. Slice the spinach and supplement the parsley mixture with it.
6. Grate Mozzarella and Parmesan cheese.
7. Add the cheese to the mixture of greenery and blend it.
8. Supplement the dough with this mixture and shape the baguette.
9. Put the dough into the Instant Pot and let it stay there for 10 minutes. You will see that the dough will rise substantially.
10. Shut the lid and turn on the "High Pressure" mode for 30 minutes.
11. Flip the meal to another side 15 minutes after the cooking has begun.
12. When the baguette is prepared, let it cool down and take it out of the pressure cooker.
13. Cut it into pieces and serve it while it is warm!

Nutrition:
- Calories: 377
- Fat: 12g
- Carbohydrates: 39g
- Protein: 27g

Exquisite Tomato Pie

This pastry is healthful and does not contain excessive fat. It is an enjoyable lunch meal for children and adults.

Prep time: 10 minutes
Cooking time: 25 minutes
Servings: 6

Ingredients:
- 9 oz. of dry tomatoes
- 7 oz. of yeast dough
- 0.5 cup of bread crumbs
- 0.25 cup of your favorite milk
- 1 egg yolk
- 2 white onions
- 2 tablespoons of butter
- 1 teaspoon of salt
- 1 teaspoon of nutmeg
- 1 teaspoon of sugar

Directions:
1. Roll out the yeast dough using a rolling pin and put it into the Instant Pot.
2. Place dry tomatoes into the dough.
3. Clear the onions from the peel, slice them and add to the dough.
4. Cover the dough with salt and sugar.
5. Supplement it with milk, nutmeg and butter.
6. Put the bread crumbs on top of that mixture.
7. Whip the egg yolk and cover the baking with it.
8. Close the lid and let the meal cook under "High Pressure" for 25 minutes.
9. Let the pressure release afterwards and be attentive when you take out the baking from the Instant Pot.
10. Now you can cut the meal into pieces and serve it.

Nutrition:
- Calories: 246
- Fat: 7g
- Carbohydrates: 35g
- Protein: 15g

Tender Sausage Pie

This pastry can be cooked beforehand and kept in the refrigerator for a couple of days. You can either prepare it in advance, or cook it and serve it right away.

Prep time: 15 minutes
Cooking time: 25 minutes
Servings: 8

Ingredients:
- 2 cups of flour
- 0.25 cup of your favorite milk
- 7 oz. of margarine
- 5 oz. of hard cheese
- 1 pound of sausages
- 1 carrot
- 1 egg
- 3 tablespoons of sour cream
- 1 teaspoon of salt
- 1 teaspoon of tomato paste
- 1 teaspoon of turmeric
- 1 teaspoon of cilantro
- 1 teaspoon of oregano

Directions:
1. Shred the margarine and mix it with flour.
2. Combine it with salt and an egg.
3. Knead the dough from the mixture. Make sure that it is soft and does not stick to your hands.
4. Slice the sausages and mix them with the tomato paste.
5. Supplement the mix with cilantro, oregano and sour cream.
6. Add some turmeric to the mixture.
7. Peel the carrot and cut it into pieces.
8. Roll out the dough to give it the shape of a circle and put it into the Instant Pot.
9. Place the sausage mix into the center of the dough and make it flat.
10. Add cut carrot and some milk to the dish.
11. Close the lid and turn on "High Pressure" mode for 25 minutes.
12. Prick the dough with a wooden stick to see if it is ready.
13. If it is cooked, take it out of the Instant Pot.
14. Cut the meal into pieces and serve it.

Nutrition:
- Calories: 535
- Fat: 33g
- Carbohydrates: 39g
- Protein: 23g

Delectable Cottage Cheese Bun

This pastry is light and cooked fast. You can easily make your family happy if you make it for a lunch!

Prep time: 15 minutes
Cooking time: 30 minutes
Servings: 6

Ingredients:
- 5 sheets of unleavened thin dough
- 1 egg yolk
- 1 cup of cottage cheese
- 1 cup of spinach
- 1 tablespoon of olive oil
- 1 tablespoon of sesame seeds
- 1 teaspoon of butter
- 1 teaspoon of oregano
- 1 teaspoon of cilantro
- 1 teaspoon of garlic dust
- 0.5 teaspoon of nutmeg

Directions:
1. Cover the sheets of dough with olive oil.
2. Take a mixing bowl and fill it with oregano, nutmeg, cilantro, garlic dust and cottage cheese.
3. Slice the spinach, add it to the mix and stir it.
4. Put the mixture on the sheets of dough and roll them to form a spiral.
5. Whip the egg yolk and cover the spiral with it.
6. Spread some sesame seeds over it and put the meal into the Instant Pot.
7. Close the lid and switch on the "High Pressure" regime for 30 minutes.
8. Take the dish out of the Instant Pot and let it cool down a little.
9. Slice it into pieces and serve the delicious meal!

Nutrition:
- Calories: 80
- Fat: 5.5g
- Carbohydrates: 4g
- Protein: 4g

Spicy Onion Rolls

These seasoned rolls are great when combined with some zesty sauce, for instance, garlic one. You can also serve them with the dipping of your choice.

Prep time: 10 minutes
Cooking time: 25 minutes
Servings: 6

Ingredients:
- 7 oz. of puff pastry
- 1 egg yolk
- 1 yellow onion
- 1 cup of shredded beef
- 2 tablespoons of water
- 1 tablespoon of cumin
- 0.5 tablespoon of lemon juice
- 1 teaspoon of olive oil
- 1 teaspoon of cilantro
- 1 teaspoon of oregano
- 1 teaspoon of salt
- 0.5 teaspoon of ginger
- 0.5 teaspoon of turmeric

Directions:
1. Put cilantro, oregano, turmeric, ginger and salt into the mixing dish.
2. Peel the onion and slice it.
3. Add onion and shredded beef to the mixture of condiments and blend it with a spoon.
4. Roll out the puff pastry and cut it into the pieces of average size.
5. Put onion mix on top of pastry pieces and form long rolls.
6. Whip the egg yolk with the water until the mass is homogenous.
7. Spread the egg mix and some cumin over the rolls.
8. Cover the Instant Pot with some olive oil on the inside and put the rolls in there.
9. Close the lid and switch on the "High Pressure" mode for 25 minutes or until the meal's readiness.
10. When ready, take it out of the pressure cooker and let it cool down for a while.
11. Now the warm dish is ready to be served!

Nutrition:
- Calories: 268
- Fat: 18g
- Carbohydrates: 17g
- Protein: 9g

Aromatic Pastry with Salmon and Vegetables

This meal is unusual and nutrient due to the salmon fillet it contains. Take time to prepare it and eat healthy!

Prep time: 15 minutes
Cooking time: 35 minutes
Servings: 6

Ingredients:
- 7 oz. of margarine
- 5 oz. of dried tomatoes
- 1 pound of boiled salmon fillet
- 2 sweet peppers
- 1 cup of flour
- 0.25 cup of garlic
- 2 tablespoons of lemon juice
- 1 tablespoon of olive oil
- 1 tablespoon of butter
- 1 teaspoon of salt
- 1 teaspoon of paprika
- 1 teaspoon of cilantro

Directions:
1. Cut the prepared fillet of salmon and cover it with salt and lemon juice. Stir the mix.
2. Shred the margarine and blend it with paprika, cilantro and flour in a mixing bowl.
3. Knead the soft dough manually.
4. Slice the dill, garlic, dried tomatoes and sweet peppers.
5. Mix the vegetables together and put them into the dish with salmon fillet.
6. Roll out the dough thoroughly.
7. Spread some olive oil inside the Instant Pot and put the dough there.
8. Cover the dough with salmon mix and make sure it is flat.
9. Wrap the sides of the dough carefully to cover the pie.
10. Turn on the "High Pressure" mode and prepare the pie for 35 minutes.
11. After it is done, let it chill, then take it out of the pressure cooker and cut it into pieces.
12. Serve the aromatic pie while it is still warm.

Nutrition:
- Calories: 550
- Fat: 37g
- Carbohydrates: 36g
- Protein: 22g

Gentle Potato and Bacon Pie

The ingredients of the pie give you the idea that it is very nourishing! Cheese and cream make it soft, and the condiments add some zest to it.

Prep time: 15 minutes
Cooking time: 30 minutes
Servings: 8

Ingredients:
- 8 oz. of bacon
- 5 oz. of Mozzarella
- 1 onion
- 1 pound of raw potatoes
- 0.5 cup of cream of your choice
- 1 tablespoon of olive oil
- 1 teaspoon of salt
- 1 teaspoon of oregano
- 1 teaspoon of cilantro
- 0.5 teaspoon of red hot chili pepper

Directions:
1. Cut the bacon into pieces and cover it with salt and cilantro. Blend the mix.
2. Wash the potatoes, peel and cut them.
3. Spread some olive oil inside the Instant Pot.
4. Place some of sliced bacon into the pressure cooker.
5. Cover it with cut potatoes, oregano and red hot chili pepper.
6. Peel the onion and dice it.
7. Shred some Mozzarella cheese.
8. Add these components into the Instant Pot and pour the cream over them.
9. Put another layer of bacon on top of all the ingredients and close the lid.
10. Turn on the "High Pressure" mode and let the meal prepare for 30 minutes.
11. Let the pressure release and see if the dish has been prepared well.
12. Take the meal out of the pressure cooker and let it cool down until it is warm.
13. Now you can slice it into as many pieces as you need and serve it with pleasure!

Nutrition:
- Calories: 200
- Fat: 13g
- Carbohydrates: 15g
- Sugar: 10g

Piquant Soup with Rice Noodles

This amazing dish is so solid that it would make great dinner, not only lunch. Those of you who love chicken meat and spices will enjoy it for sure!

Prep time: 15 minutes
Cooking time: 31 minutes
Servings: 9

Ingredients:
- 4 oz. of green onion
- 3 oz. of shallot
- 4 oz. of rice noodles
- 2 pounds of chicken breast
- 2 onions of average size
- 0.5 of lime
- 5 cups of beef stock
- 0.3 cup of fresh basil
- 1 tablespoon of garlic sauce
- 0.5 tablespoon of ground chili pepper
- 1 teaspoon of ground white pepper
- 1 teaspoon of paprika
- 1 teaspoon of salt
- 1 teaspoon of nutmeg

Directions:
1. Peel the onions, cut them and put them into the Instant Pot.
2. Slice the shallot and green onion and put them into the pressure cooker as well.
3. Cover the mix with ground white and chili pepper, nutmeg, paprika and salt.
4. Blend the mix and turn on the "Sauté" regime for half a minute.
5. When this is done, add beef stock and chicken breast into the Instant Pot.
6. Close the lid and let the dish prepare under "High Pressure" for 30 minutes.
7. After that let the pressure release and take the chicken meat out of the broth.
8. Drain the beef stock into serving bowls using the colander.
9. Grate the chicken meat and add it to every serving.
10. Put rice noodles into every serving dish.
11. Add some garlic sauce to the meal as well.
12. Squeeze out some juice from the lime over each serving. This will make the meal more sour.
13. Stir the dish with care and feel free to serve it.

Nutrition:
- Calories: 225
- Fat: 10g
- Carbohydrates: 9g
- Protein: 24g

Delicate Pie with Asparagus

This fragrant pie will be wonderful with tea or your favorite drink. It does not contain sugar and has a fragrant vegetable flavor.

Prep time: 15 minutes
Cooking time: 30 minutes
Servings: 6

Ingredients:
- 1 pound of asparagus
- 1 egg
- 10 oz. of margarine
- 3 cups of flour
- 0.5 cup of dill
- 0.5 cup of bread crumbs
- 2 tablespoons of olive oil
- 1 tablespoon of butter
- 1 teaspoon of paprika
- 1 teaspoon of salt

Directions:
1. Beat an egg into the mixing dish.
2. Complete it with flour and margarine. Make sure that margarine is not frozen but soft.
3. Mix the components and knead the dough.
4. Put butter into the pressure cooker and let it melt down.
5. Slice the dill and asparagus and mix the vegetables.
6. Cover the mix with bread crumbs, paprika and salt. Blend it well.
7. Place the dough into the Instant Pot and make it flat.
8. Cover it with the asparagus blend and the bread crumbs with condiments.
9. Spread some olive oil over the dish and shut the lid.
10. Let the meal cook under "High Pressure" for half an hour.
11. When the time is up, let the pressure release and the baking cool down.
12. Slice the pastry into pieces and enjoy it with your family!

Nutrition:
- Calories: 660
- Fat: 47g
- Carbohydrates: 53g
- Protein: 10g

Creamy Bean Soup

This soup with soft beans and juicy chicken is irresistible! The valuable vegetables will fill your body with vitamins and energy.

Prep time: 15 minutes
Cooking time: 55 minutes
Servings: 8

Ingredients:
- 1 pound of chicken fillet
- 1 white onion
- 1 red sweet pepper
- 1 jalapeno pepper
- 7 cups of water
- 1 cup of cannellini beans
- 1 cup of dill
- 0.3 cup of cream
- 4 tablespoons of salsa
- 2 teaspoons of salt
- 1 teaspoon of soy sauce
- 1 teaspoon of white pepper

Directions:
1. Put the cannellini beans into the Instant Pot.
2. Slice the chicken fillet and put it into the Instant Pot.
3. Cover the meal with water and let the beans prepare under "High Pressure" for 35 minutes.
4. While the beans are being cooked, slice the dill and jalapeno pepper, onion and red sweet pepper.
5. When the time is up, complete the bean mix with these vegetables and close the lid.
6. Turn on the "Soup" regime for 15 more minutes.
7. Add cream, salsa, white pepper and soy sauce to the soup.
8. Blend the soup with care and let it prepare for 5 more minutes.
9. Upon readiness, take it out of the pressure cooker and set it aside for it to cool down slightly.
10. Now feel free to pour soup into serving dishes.

Nutrition:
- Calories: 190
- Fat: 10g
- Carbohydrates: 17g
- Protein: 7g

Heavenly Cauliflower Pastry

This gentle vegetable baking is another meal that the Instant Pot can help you with. The pie with cheese and cream is a tasty lunch indeed.

Prep time: 15 minutes
Cooking time: 25 minutes
Servings: 8

Ingredients:
- 7 oz. of unleavened dough sheets
- 8 oz. of hard cheese of your choice (possibly Parmesan)
- 1 pound cauliflower head
- 7 eggs
- 2 tablespoons of butter
- 1 tablespoon of olive oil
- 1 tablespoon of paprika
- 1 tablespoon of salt
- 0.3 cup of cottage cheese
- 0.25 cup of cream
- 0.5 teaspoon of nutmeg

Directions:
1. Clean the cauliflower thoroughly and tear it into florets.
2. Slice them finely and cover them with salt.
3. Beat the eggs into a bowl and whip them.
4. Complete them with cottage cheese and paprika and stir the mix.
5. Supplement the mixture with nutmeg and cream and blend it well.
6. Unite cauliflower with all the other mixed ingredients.
7. Spread some olive oil on the dough sheets and put them into the Instant Pot.
8. Put the layer of cauliflower mix on the dough.
9. Close the lid and use "High Pressure" regime for 25 minutes.
10. When you know that the pastry is cooked, let the pressure release and take the dish out when it is not too hot.
11. After the meal is cut into pieces, it is ready for serving.

Nutrition:
- Calories: 400
- Fat: 27g
- Carbohydrates: 21g
- Protein: 19g

Juicy Salad with Baked Apples and Turkey

Sweet baked apples reveal the flavor of turkey meat amazingly well! We advise that you taste this lunch dish as soon as you can.

Prep time: 15 minutes
Cooking time: 30 minutes
Servings: 8

Ingredients:
- 7 oz. of red sweet apples
- 8 oz. of turkey fillet
- 2 cucumbers
- 0.5 lime
- 1 cup of arugula
- 0.5 cup of lettuce
- 0.25 cup of walnuts
- 2 tablespoons of orange juice
- 1 tablespoon of sesame seeds
- 1 tablespoon of apple cider vinegar
- 1 tablespoon of mustard
- 1 teaspoon of honey
- 1 teaspoon of butter
- 1 teaspoon of sesame oil
- 0.5 teaspoon of ground black pepper

Directions:
1. Cover the turkey fillet with vinegar, ground black pepper and mustard. Mix the blend.
2. Put the meat into the Instant Pot.
3. Complete it with butter and let it cook for 25 minutes under "High Pressure".
4. Take the meat from the pressure cooker when the time is up. Let it cool down.
5. Cover the apples with honey and walnuts.
6. Put them into the Instant Pot and let them cook for 5 minutes under "High Pressure".
7. Take the fruits out of the pressure cooker and let them chill.
8. Wash the lettuce and arugula, tear them into pieces and place them into the mixing dish.
9. Slice the cucumbers and add them to the salad.
10. Complete the salad with sesame oil.
11. Press some lime juice out of the lime to dress the salad.
12. Slice the baked apples and turkey, and supplement the salad with these components.
13. Add sesame seeds and orange juice to the salad and blend it with a wooden spoon.
14. Serve the delicious meal all at once!

Nutrition:
- Calories: 200
- Fat: 16g
- Carbohydrates: 7g
- Protein: 7g

Fried Rice with Pineapple

Delicious pineapple gives special flavor to the meal. The combination of ham, rice and eggs tastes great!

Prep time: 10 minutes
Cooking time: 30 minutes
Servings: 6

Ingredients:
- 6 oz. of cooked ham, sliced in cubes
- 3 eggs, scrambled slightly
- 1 little onion
- 1 sweet red pepper, sliced
- Sliced scallions
- 2 cups of water
- 1 cup of sliced pineapple
- 1.5 cups of unprepared brown rice, washed and rinsed
- 2 tablespoons of soy sauce
- 1 tablespoon of olive oil

Directions:
1. Put the onion, olive oil and sweet red pepper into the Instant Pot and turn on the "Sauté" regime.
2. Remember to stir the vegetables while they are being stewed.
3. When you see that the onion and pepper have become soft, complete the dish with ham and keep stirring.
4. Complete the mixture with eggs and blend them for a couple of minutes until they are prepared.
5. Supplement the dish with brown rice, soy sauce, water and sliced pineapple.
6. Close the lid and turn on the "Manual" mode.
7. Set the time for 24 minutes and switch on "High Pressure" option.
8. When the time has passed, let the rice linger in the Instant Pot in "Keep Warm" regime for 5 more minutes.
9. After that time open the pressure cooker and put the rice into serving bowls.
10. Use sliced scallions as garnish for your servings.
11. Enjoy the meal!

Nutrition:
- Calories: 556
- Fat: 24.4g
- Carbohydrates: 67.4g
- Protein: 21.4g
- Cholesterol: 194 mg

Delightful Pasta with Cheese and Milk

This dish is as luscious, as it is simple. Mild and cheesy macaroni are pure pleasure to taste!

Prep time: 15 minutes
Cooking time: 4 minutes
Servings: 8

Ingredients:
- 1 pound of macaroni or dry pasta shells
- 1 can of evaporated milk
- 8 oz. of grated extra sharp Cheddar cheese
- 8 oz. of grated Monterey Jack cheese
- 3 or 4 dashes of hot pepper sauce
- 4 cups of water
- 2 tablespoons of butter
- 1 tablespoon of salt
- 1 tablespoon of mustard

Directions:
1. Put water, dry pasta, butter, hot pepper sauce, mustard and salt into the bowl inserted into the Instant Pot.
2. Close the lid and switch on "High Pressure" manual regime for 4 minutes.
3. When the 4 minutes countdown has finished, use quick pressure release and turn of the Instant Pot. Make sure that the "Keep Warm" regime is not turned on, because pasta should not be overcooked.
4. When the pressure has been released, open the lid and blend the milk into the meal.
5. Afterwards stir in the grated cheese of both kinds.
6. Keep stirring the dish until the cheese has fully melted.
7. If you want to serve the meal later, turn on the "Keep warm" regime.
8. In case you would like to serve it all at once, go ahead and do it.

Nutrition:
- Calories: 582
- Fat: 33g
- Carbohydrates: 47.8g
- Protein: 24.3g
- Cholesterol: 95 mg

Enjoyable Chicken and Noodles

The savory sauce and rice noodles are a great combination! Feel free to garnish this dish with greenery, peanuts or condiments.

Prep time: 5 minutes
Cooking time: 35 minutes
Servings: 5

Ingredients:
- 1.5 pound of chicken breasts, without skin and bones
- 1 cup of Thai peanut sauce
- 1 cup of sugar snap peas or snow peas
- 0.75 cup of chicken stock
- 5 oz. of rice noodles
- Crashed peanuts, green onions, cilantro and grated red pepper – if desired

Directions:
1. Place the peas into your Instant Pot and turn on the "Sauté" mode for 1 or 2 minutes. Let the peas cook just a little bit.
2. Take the peas out and set them aside. Turn off the "Sauté" regime.
3. Transfer the chicken breasts, Thai peanut sauce and chicken stock into the Instant Pot.
4. Switch on the "High Pressure" mode and let the meal cook for 12 minutes.
5. When the steam has been released, take the chicken meat from the pressure cooker. Drain it and let the sauce remain in the Instant Pot.
6. Complete the sauce with rice noodles and make sure the noodles are covered well.
7. Cover the meal with peas and turn on the "Normal" setting of Instant Pot's slow cooker option. Let the meal cook for approximately 10 minutes. Keep in mind that the noodles do not need to be too soft.
8. Grate the chicken breasts and set them aside.
9. Open the lid when the noodles are done and stir them.
10. Put the chicken back into the pressure cooker and let it cook for 10 more minutes at the same mode.
11. Serve the meal while it is warm!

Nutrition:
- Calories: 417
- Fat: 5.6g
- Carbohydrates: 54.4g
- Protein: 36.9g
- Cholesterol: 65 mg

Cheesy Pasta with Meat

This pasta will be amazing when served hot! The rich and nourishing dish will satisfy the most demanding taste.

Prep time: 2 minutes
Cooking time: 5 minutes
Servings: 4

Ingredients:
- 16 oz. of ruffle shaped pasta
- 8 oz. of Mozzarella cheese
- 8 oz. of Ricotta cheese
- 32 oz. of Jar Pasta sauce
- 32 oz. of water
- 0.5 pound of shredded beef
- 0.5 pound of shredded sausage

Directions:
1. Turn on the "Sauté" regime of the Instant Pot.
2. Place shredded beef and sausage into the pressure cooker and prepare them until they have browned up.
3. Complete the dish with pasta, water and sauce.
4. Upon doing so, switch on the "High Pressure" option of "Manual" regime and cook the meal for 5 minutes.
5. Use a quick method of pressure release when the time is up.
6. Take the meal out, put it into a bowl and switch off the Instant Pot.
7. Complete the dish by stirring in the grated Ricotta cheese and a part of Mozzarella cheese.
8. Pour the meal onto the baking pan and cover it with the remaining Mozzarella cheese.
9. Let the dish bake until the cheese has melted.
10. Serve the meal when it is ready.

Nutrition:
- Calories: 744
- Fat: 36.1g
- Carbohydrates: 51.5g
- Protein: 50.8g

Savory Sandwiches with Beef and Cheese

These homemade sandwiches are rich in taste and value. You can have them for lunch at home or wrap them up and enjoy them in the nature.

Prep time: 5 minutes
Cooking time: 15 minutes
Servings: 8

Ingredients:
- 10.75 oz. of chicken gumbo soup, drained partially
- 10.75 oz. of tomato soup
- 2 pound of shredded beef
- 3 sliced green onions
- 8 pieces of American cheese
- Sandwich buns, divided in halves
- 2 tablespoons of mustard
- 1 tablespoon of ketchup
- 0.5 teaspoon of salt
- 0.25 teaspoon of ground black pepper

Directions:
1. Switch on the Instant Pot and choose the "Sauté" option.
2. Fill the pressure cooker with shredded beef and cook it at medium heat with the lid removed.
3. Watch for the beef to brown up. When it is ready, press the "Cancel" button to stop the "Sauté" mode and drain the beef.
4. Put the rest of the components except for the buns and cheese into the Instant Pot.
5. Cover them with the lid and turn on the "Manual" regime under "High Pressure". Let the meal prepare for 7 minutes.
6. When it is done, choose a quick pressure release method.
7. Cover the halves of sandwich buns with beef mix and put cheese slices on top of it.
8. Complete the sandwiches with the other bread halves and serve them.

Nutrition:
- Calories: 578
- Fat: 17.4g
- Carbohydrates: 66.7g
- Protein: 41.5g
- Cholesterol: 93 mg

FREE BONUS GIFT!

Dear friend!
Thank you so much for buying my book and supporting my next cookbooks which I hope you will enjoy as well. In order to thank you I am very happy to present you a gift set of 5 cookbooks.

Please follow this link to get instant access and DOWNLOAD your BONUS:
goo.gl/v5wyHg
(No subscription or other additional actions required)

Copyright 2017 by - All rights reserved.

All rights Reserved. No part of this publication or the information in it may be quoted from or reproduced in any form by means such as printing, scanning, photocopying or otherwise without prior written permission of the copyright holder.

Disclaimer and Terms of Use: Effort has been made to ensure that the information in this book is accurate and complete, however, the author and the publisher do not warrant the accuracy of the information, text and graphics contained within the book due to the rapidly changing nature of science, research, known and unknown facts and internet. The Author and the publisher do not hold any responsibility for errors, omissions or contrary interpretation of the subject matter herein. This book is presented solely for motivational and informational purposes only.

www.ingramcontent.com/pod-product-compliance
Lightning Source LLC
LaVergne TN
LVHW060144070326
832902LV00018B/2941